Mixed-Media Master Class

with Sherrill Kahn

50+ Surface-Design Techniques for Fabric & Paper

C&T PUBLISHING

Text copyright © 2013 by Sherrill Kahn

Photography and Artwork copyright © 2013 by C&T Publishing, Inc.

PUBLISHER: Amy Marson

CREATIVE DIRECTOR: Gailen Runge

ART DIRECTOR: Kristy Zacharias

EDITOR: Lynn Koolish

TECHNICAL EDITOR: Gailen Runge

COVER/BOOK DESIGNER: April Mostek

PRODUCTION COORDINATOR: Jessica Jenkins

PRODUCTION EDITORS: S. Michele Fry and Joanna Burgarino

PHOTOGRAPHY by Cara Pardo, Christina Carty-Francis, and
Diane Pedersen of C&T Publishing, Inc., unless otherwise noted

Published by C&T Publishing, Inc., P.O. Box 1456, Lafayette, CA 94549

Library of Congress Cataloging-in-Publication Data

Kahn, Sherrill, 1941-

  Mixed-media master class with Sherrill Kahn : 50+ surface-design techniques for fabric & paper / Sherrill Kahn.

    pages cm

  ISBN 978-1-60705-423-8 (soft cover)

  1. Art--Technique. I. Title.

  N7430.5.K335 2013

  702.81--dc23

                    2012030336

Printed in China

10 9 8 7 6 5 4 3 2 1

DEDICATION

I love writing books and could not do so without the continuing support of my precious husband, Joel. He builds me up when I get discouraged or a project just doesn't turn out the way I had hoped. He is always there for me.

I also love to teach, and again I thank Joel so much for supporting this passion, since it takes me from home many months of the year.

ACKNOWLEDGMENTS

I want to thank all of the people at C&T Publishing for helping me write this book.

Lynn Koolish—the editor. Lynn has been so supportive and has given me invaluable advice along the path to this finished book. I couldn't have written this book without her.

Gailen Runge—the technical editor. Her sharp eyes made sure that everything was clear and correct.

April Mostek—the book designer. April has made a book that is exactly what I would have dreamed it to be. I love what she has done.

Diane Pederson—the photographer. Diane has created beautiful photographs of my artwork. She was patient during a very long 2-day shoot of all of the step-by-step shots. She shot 1,000 photos in the 2 days.

Cara Pardo—the photography assistant. She gathered all of the supplies for the photo shoot and was invaluable for the 2 days I was at C&T.

Jessica Jenkins—the production coordinator, and Joanna Burgarino—the production editor. Together they kept the book on track and followed through with all the final details to get this book to the printer.

Contents

Introduction:
Using This Book

This book is designed to help you explore many easy and fun mixed-media techniques. I hope that when trying each technique you'll think, "What if I try doing this on a different surface or with different media?" Take your idea and see how it works and if it leads you to other ideas and techniques. I've developed many of my techniques by asking, "What if …?" and just trying things out. One thing inevitably leads to another. You will like some of the techniques more than others. Keep exploring those techniques to see where they lead you in your design process.

Have fun and don't worry about making masterpieces. Think about creating fabric and paper that will be cut up or torn to be used in larger works—don't worry if every part of a piece of paper or fabric isn't perfect. You can select and use the portions that work for you. The examples in this book, especially in Putting It All Together (pages 131), will give you some great ideas on combining and collaging.

Tip: Make a Print!

Many of the techniques presented in this book involve the liberal use of paints and inks—so liberal that you may have excess paint and ink either on your fabric or paper or on your work surface. There's never a reason to waste, so make a print.

Simply place a piece of fabric or paper on the excess paint or ink and press down with your hands or a brayer. Lift up the paper or fabric and you have a print. You may even be able to make several prints, one right after the other.

Materials and Supplies

First of all—don't panic! You don't need everything on these lists. These are the things that I used to create *all* the examples for *all* the techniques in this book. Some of the things you'll have already, and most of the others are easy to get. Feel free to make substitutes as you make the techniques in this book your own.

From the Art Supply Store
✓ Acrylic paint or fabric paint
✓ Assorted paintbrushes
✓ Brayer
✓ Craft tissue such as Spectra Bleeding Art Tissue
✓ Dorland's Wax
✓ Fun foam
✓ Gesso
✓ Inktense pencils and blocks
✓ Liquid wax / Jacquard Water-Based Resist
✓ Matte gel medium
✓ Metal or plastic stencils
✓ Metal tape
✓ Oil pastels
✓ Rubber stamps
✓ Silkscreens (blank)
✓ Soft (chalk) pastels

From around the House

✓ Eyedroppers or pipettes

✓ Hair gel

✓ Nails

✓ Old credit cards

✓ Petroleum jelly

✓ Rubber bands

✓ Rubbing alcohol

✓ Single-edge razor blade

✓ Sponge squares

✓ Spray bottle

✓ Styrofoam

✓ Takeout knives and forks

✓ White candle

From the Office Supply Store

✓ Blue gluesticks

✓ Masking tape

✓ Permanent markers

✓ Wax crayons (I prefer Twist-Up from Staples.)

✓ Water-soluble markers

✓ White glue such as Elmer's School Glue

From the Hardware Store

✓ 3"–4" PVC pipe, 12" long

✓ Notched spreader/scraper

✓ Rock salt

✓ Wallboard grid

Other (see Resources, page 143)

✓ Gelli Plates

✓ Impress Me rubber stamps

✓ Thermofax screens

SURFACES

A wonderful thing has happened in recent years—more and more interesting surfaces have appeared in our art and craft stores, and it is fun to explore them all. A trip to a home improvement store, stationery store, or fabric store will yield other possibilities for working on different surfaces.

Below are some possible surfaces for you to explore; all of them are absorbent, with the exception of photo paper.

Papers

✓ **From around the house:** Coffee filters, deli or sandwich wrap, newspaper, paper bags, tea bags, wrapping paper, any kind of paper you think might add to the experience

✓ **From the art supply store:** Bristol board, colored tissue paper, canvas board, illustration board, rice paper, watercolor paper

✓ **From the office supply or warehouse store:** Copy paper, card stock, photo paper (I prefer Kirkland from Costco), envelopes

Fabrics/Fibers

Cottons of all types (white, black, solid, and printed), rayons, silks, cheesecloth, knits, polyesters, cotton/poly blends, interfacing in different weights, quilt batting

Other Surfaces

Lutradur, mul-tex, Transfer Artist Paper (TAP)

Creating Surfaces

Cheesecloth

I have found that the word *cheesecloth* can apply to a variety of soft nettings. Most cheesecloth is close in weave, and all types seem to love being painted and dyed and used in creative artwork. You can also use gauze.

Cheesecloth can be sewn or glued (with matte gel medium or other heavy glue) to a surface before painting it if desired. You can find cheesecloth in hardware stores and markets.

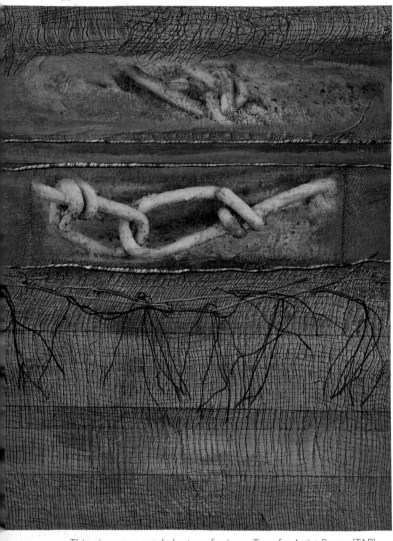

This piece was made by transferring a Transfer Artist Paper (TAP) image (page 25) to illustration board. Then paint, cheesecloth, and eyelash yarn were added. Layers of acrylic washes (page 35) were applied to finish the design.

A variety of materials were collaged to illustration board, and then paint and cheesecloth were added. Layers of acrylic washes (page 35) were applied to finish the design.

This composition combines a number of collaged pieces with rubber stamping (page 111) and colored pencil on a plain piece of illustration board. After I collaged the pieces, I painted the Prussian blue color around the perimeter of the artwork. To finish the piece, I glued dyed cheesecloth to the left of the central piece.

HOW-TO

1. Glue cheesecloth to the chosen surface.

2. Paint the cheesecloth with liquid paint or dye.

3. Add other embellishments as desired.

Cloth Paper—Glue Paper to Fabric or Fabric to Paper

Many articles have been written about creating cloth paper. The process, which was invented by Beryl Taylor, has become very popular, and truly this technique is addictive. The possibilities are endless, since you can glue layers of thin and thick papers onto cloth, paint the piece later, or use it for collage. If it isn't too thick, you can sew through it. You also can glue commercial fabrics or preprinted or painted fabrics to paper. Whatever the method, you are creating cloth paper.

I use matte gel medium to glue the various elements together.

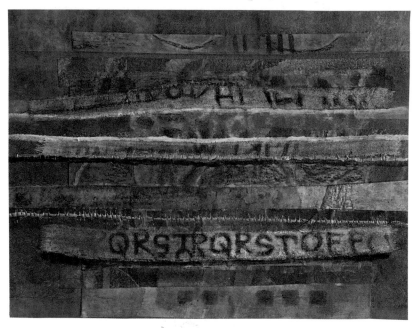

This piece of cloth paper incorporates a variety of papers, including stenciled letters. I used Jacquard's applicator-tipped paint to highlight two areas with a horizontal line.

Various rice papers and commercial papers glued to fabric

Various pieces of painted sandwich (or deli) paper glued to white cotton fabric

This composition was created by collaging a series of papers, including cloth paper and deli paper, to a piece of illustration board. I coordinated the design by layering diluted acrylic washes (page 35) over selected areas. I used various colored pencils to emphasize areas and create a stronger composition after the paint had dried. The colored pencil areas that stand out are the strong red-orange areas.

HOW-TO

1. Coat a layer of paper with matte gel medium or glue thick enough to secure the paper to a piece of fabric. The fabric can be plain, colored, or patterned.

2. Apply a second layer of paper with glue.

3. Repeat as needed.

Various pieces of painted sandwich (or deli) paper glued to white cotton fabric

Copy Paper

When I work, I put one or two pieces of copy paper under the piece I'm creating. When I do washes on fabric, the color goes through to the copy paper. I can build layers of color on the copy paper and then tear the edges of the painted areas into creative shapes for collage. This is a very easy technique that sometimes produces breathtaking results.

Multiple colors were painted on thin cotton fabric and allowed to soak onto copy paper placed beneath the fabric.

This sample has colored pencil added to selected areas of the painted copy paper.

HOW-TO

1. Place several pieces of copy paper under a piece of fabric. Wet the fabric, and use wet-into-wet techniques (page 77).

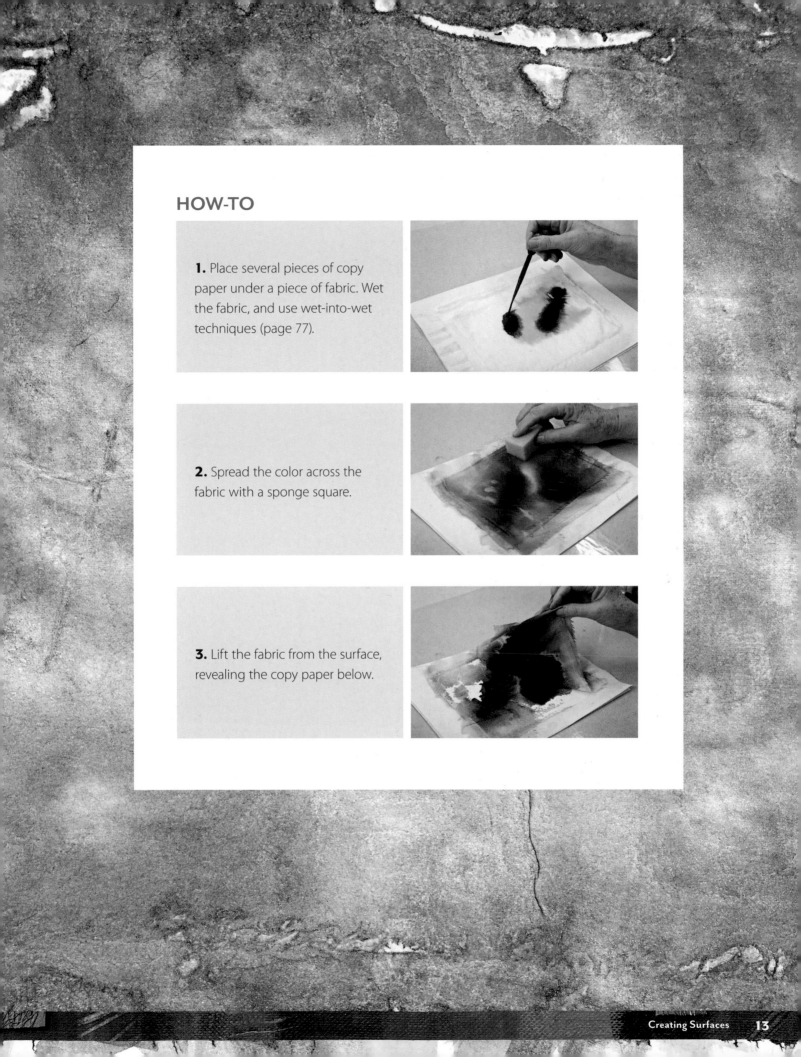

2. Spread the color across the fabric with a sponge square.

3. Lift the fabric from the surface, revealing the copy paper below.

Copy Paper Texture

This process is one of my favorites, and my students love it as well. It can be used on any copy paper, even copy paper that's been printed on. It can be sewn, collaged, and used for any number of projects.

These samples were made from machine-stitched, painted, crumpled, dried, and ironed copy paper, with each layer added to build the final design. Additional elements include ironed fabric cord (page 16), painted silk and cotton, and thin papers.

Multiple layers of copy paper were glued to a stiff surface and painted with layers of color. The diagonal line is a fabric cord (page 16). Air-dried clay embellishments complete the design.

HOW-TO

1. Apply paint and paint washes onto a piece of copy paper. Try using copy paper from your printer that you would otherwise throw out. As an alternative, painter's paper (olive green to brown paper sold in rolls at home improvement stores) works well.

2. Crumple the wet paper.

3. Carefully uncrumple the paper and let it dry; then iron it flat.

Special Technique: Making Fabric Cord

Fabric cord is a wonderful dimensional element to add to paper or fabric collages. Two ways to make it are shown on the pages that follow. After the cord is dry, paint it as needed. Use heavy glue or matte gel medium to glue the cord to a paper or fabric surface. You may need to cover the cord with a piece of freezer paper and weigh it down with books to keep it in place until the glue dries.

Very thin papers can also be used to create paper cords in the same manner as the fabric cords.

MAKING FABRIC CORD USING GLUE

1. Tear a piece of painted or commercial fabric into a strip approximately ³⁄₈″–½″ wide.

2. Cut the fabric to the desired length.

3. Squeeze a line of white glue or fabric glue down the middle of the fabric.

4. Twist the fabric into a cord by hand.

Note: You will get a lot of glue on your fingers, so wash your hands as soon as possible so that you don't get glue on other surfaces.

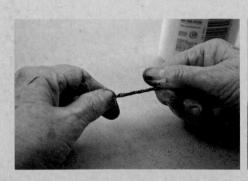

MAKING FABRIC CORD BY IRONING

If you don't want to use glue and your fabric is thin enough, you can wet the fabric and iron it while rolling it under the tip of the iron.

1. Wet the fabric thoroughly.

2. Begin rolling the fabric.

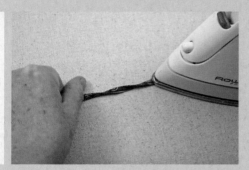

3. Continue rolling and ironing until the fabric is dry.

Craft Tissue—Water Spotted

I learned this technique years ago from a friend. It is a fun and effective way to create wonderful colored papers to use in collages.

For this piece, I tore dry pieces of water-spotted tissue into strips and odd shapes to create a collage. Then I glued a variety of colors together into one composition on a small canvas board. I glazed (page 35) two vertical strips with an ochre color and, while the paint was wet, scratched into the wet paint with the hard end of the brush, creating a repetition of horizontal lines. I sealed the final piece with matte medium so that the colors wouldn't run.

I created these pieces by placing three to five different colors of craft tissue one on top of another. I lightly sprinkled water through all the layers and added even more water spots. The bleeding of the colors through the layers created interesting papers to use for collage.

HOW-TO

1. Stack layers of different colors of craft tissue paper on top of each other. You may use from 3 to 5 different colors at a time. Try dark, medium, and light colors together.

2. Drop water onto the tissue with an eyedropper. The color will spread through the layers.

3. Repeat as desired.

Tip

Another way to use the tissue is to place either water-spotted or right-from-the-package tissue on the chosen surface, mist it with water, and remove it after the colors have bled onto the surface.

Inkjet Images—Water Spotted

This is a fun technique because you don't know how the piece will turn out until you're finished. When you spray a fresh inkjet print, the ink bleeds. The more spray you apply, the larger the water spots. This technique works best on images on paper, but it can also be used on fabric. **Note:** The key is to spray immediately after the print comes out of the printer.

This collage incorporates a variety of elements. The background is composed of water-spotted digital images. I glued additional copy paper collage strips (page 12) vertically over the background. I glazed the copy paper with acrylic washes (page 35) and painted parallel lines of cool colors on the strips. To finish the piece, I glued on strips of grass cloth wallpaper and glazed them with cool washes to coordinate with the rest of the collage.

HOW-TO

1. Spray water on a fresh inkjet print and allow it to dry.

2. Seal dried images on paper with matte medium. Fabric images do not need to be sealed.

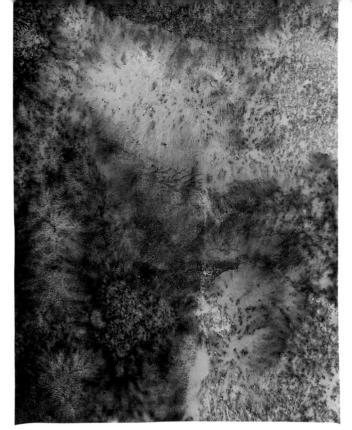
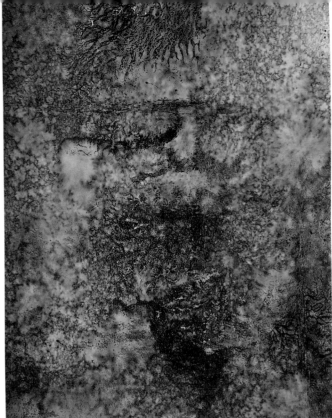

These pieces use digital images on photo paper sprayed with water immediately after printing, allowing the images to bleed. A fine mist produces tiny water spots; heavy sprays make large spots.

These pieces were created by printing an image on fabric with an inkjet printer and spritzing it with water. The technique is the same as spraying inkjet images that are printed on photo paper, but the effect is very different because the fabric is absorbent and the ink bleeds rather than spotting.

Lutradur

Lutradur is an amazing product. I am totally in love with the possibilities presented by its strength, texture, and versatility. It is 100% nonwoven polyester. It can take heat transfers (such as Transfer Artist Paper, page 25), can be sewn, and loves to be drawn on with colored pencil. I have also used paint and oil pastels on the surface, and both adhere beautifully. It can be melted and cut into with a heat tool for added textural effects.

You can coat Lutradur with matte medium and use it in an inkjet printer. After the print sets for about twenty minutes, coat it with matte medium so the inkjet color doesn't run. For more ideas on using Lutradur, take a look at the book *Fabulous Fabric Art with Lutradur* by Lesley Riley.

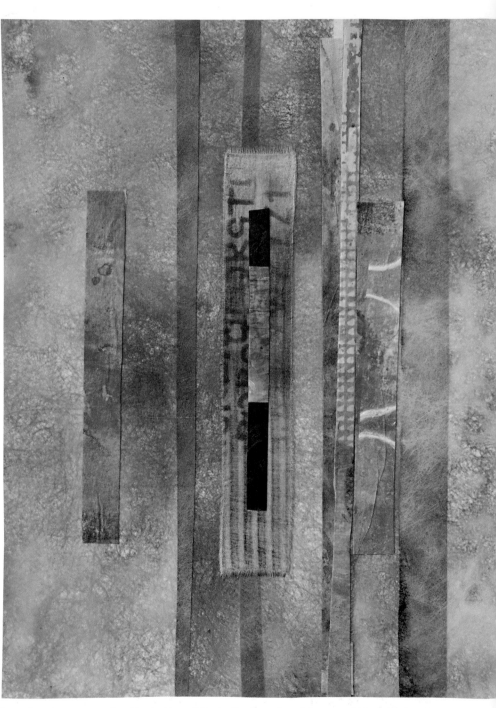

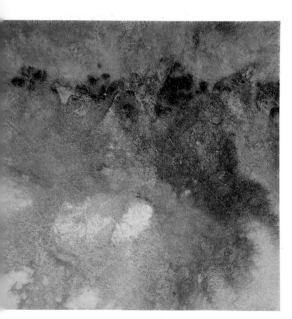

In this piece, lutradur was painted with acrylic washes, gesso, and metallic gold. The Lutradur fibers add to the pleasing design surface.

Lutradur pieces were glued to a piece of illustration board, and then washes of color were applied to the background. Additional pieces of Lutradur, thin pieces of fabric paper (page 10), and collage elements were added.

Layers of painted Lutradur were collaged to stiff illustration board. Additional paint washes (page 35) were added to make a more compelling composition. Oil pastel glazing (page 32) was added for depth.

This is a more complex composition using layers of Lutradur on Kirkland photo paper in various colors and textures. Darks were added with oil pastel glazing techniques (page 32).

HOW-TO

1. Spray the Lutradur with water and paint washes of color onto the surface.

2. Add other colors and manipulate the paint as desired (in this example I used the end of a hard brush handle).

3. Add a wash of white gesso with a flat brush.

4. Scrape into the gesso with the wooden end of the brush.

Tip

When working with Lutradur, be sure to put paper or fabric underneath because the Lutradur is porous, and color going through to the layers underneath creates additional fabric or paper that you can use.

If there is excess paint on the surface, be sure to take a print.

Transfer Artist Paper (TAP)

I absolutely love TAP and see all types of incredible possibilities for using it in creative work. It is a wonderful transfer paper developed by mixed-media artist Lesley Riley, who also wrote an excellent book—*Create with Transfer Artist Paper*.

The process is easy. You can draw, paint, or print an inkjet image on TAP. Iron the TAP onto the chosen surface—there are many possibilities to explore. You can tear or cut TAP into smaller elements for your work. If you are tearing, tear from the wrong side to prevent flaking on the edge of the TAP. TAP can be scratched easily before being used, so keep it protected in a plastic sleeve until you are ready to use it in your work.

TIPS ON USING TAP

✓ Refer to the TAP package for detailed instructions on using the product.

✓ Use a needle tool to lift the edge of the TAP immediately after ironing it to the surface.

✓ After the TAP is transferred to the surface it can be stitched, crumpled for texture, collaged, painted, and colored with the media of your choice.

✓ The polymer coating on the TAP is easy to scratch before it is transferred. Be careful not to accidentally scratch the surface—or take advantage of this characteristic and scratch a design element in your work.

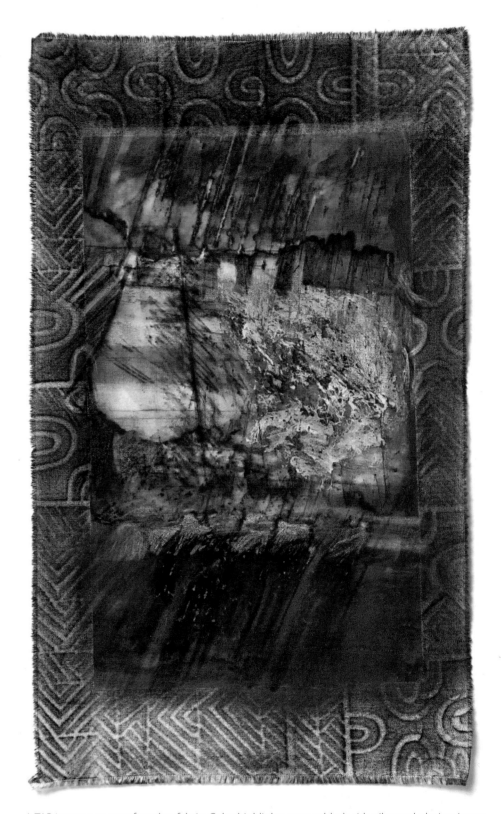

A TAP image was transferred to fabric. Color highlights were added with oil pastel glazing (page 32) over Impress Me rubber stamps. Additional oil pastels glazes were added to select areas of the design to create a stronger composition (page 32).

HOW-TO

1. Print the image on TAP.

2. Scratch areas of the TAP before ironing and transferring it to the chosen surface if desired; otherwise transfer the image without altering it. (Refer to the TAP packaging for instructions on transferring.)

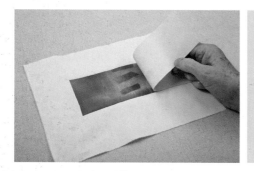

3. Add oil pastel glazing, acrylic washes, colored pencil, collage, or any other technique to enhance the TAP image.

TAP images were transferred to white fabric, and additional color was applied with acrylic washes (page 35), colored pencils, and oil pastel glazing (page 32).

A TAP image was torn into four pieces and glued to a piece of painted cardstock.

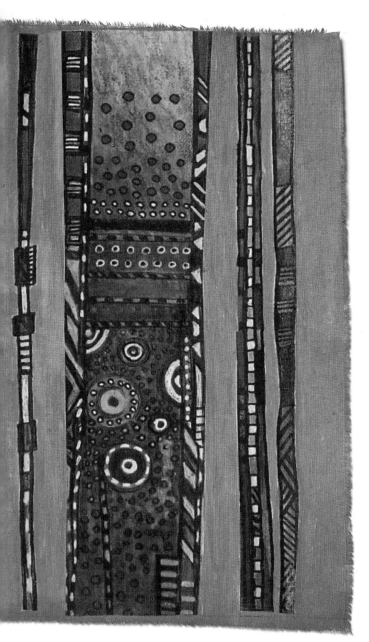

Transferred TAP images were glued to illustration board, and the slate blue background was painted to make the TAP pieces stand out.

A TAP image was transferred to fabric, and color highlights were added with oil pastel glazing (page 32), rubbing (page 84), and stenciling (page 75).

Media

Chalk Pastels + Matte Medium

This is an amazing and simple technique. By using very inexpensive chalk pastels, which are easily found in art and craft stores, you can create a thick, flat paint or a thinner, flat glaze of color. All you need is a single-edged razor blade or a sharp scraping tool, matte medium (or other medium you wish to use), palette paper, and a brush and water.

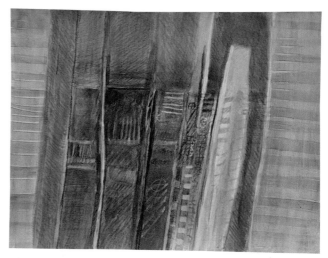

This piece was created by painting a piece of illustration board with acrylic matte medium mixed with soft pastel scrapings. The wet surfaces were scratched with the end of a wooden brush handle.

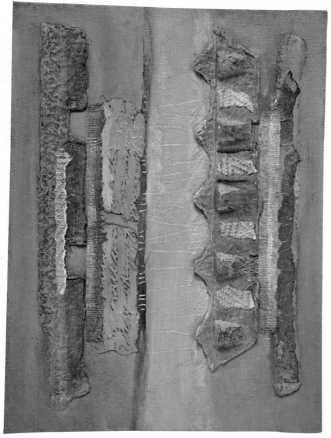

Cardboard egg carton shapes were the basis of the relief pieces used in this design. They were torn from the egg carton and cut into various shapes. A neutral background was painted on a piece of illustration board before the painted egg carton pieces were collaged to the surface. Additional paint was added to the piece, and some areas were scratched through to reveal the colors below. Additional collage elements were added to create the finished composition.

This piece, which combines painting and collage, was created on illustration board. Layers of color were painted on the board first, and then collage pieces were created and added to the design. Additional painted areas were also added. Two rubber-stamped images from my rubber stamp catalog were collaged to the surface and subdued with muted color. Additional paint colors were added to the composition to make a stronger finished piece.

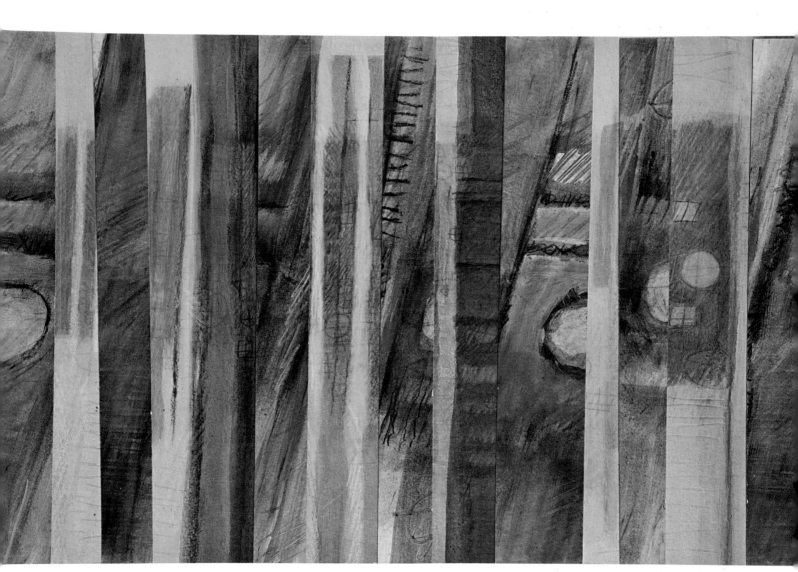

Layers of color were created by adding acrylic matte medium mixed with scrapings of soft pastel colors; wet surfaces were scratched with the end of a wooden brush handle.

Layers of color were created by adding acrylic matte medium mixed with scrapings of soft pastel colors; wet surfaces were scratched with the end of a wooden brush handle.

HOW-TO

1. Shave soft pastel color onto a piece of palette paper using a single-edged razor blade. Add additional color or colors as needed.

2. Mix matte medium with the powdered shavings until you are satisfied with the color. Brush water into the mix if the paint is too stiff to paint onto the chosen surface.

3. Apply the color to the chosen surface and if desired, while the paint is wet, scrape into it with a brush handle, scraping tool, or embossing tool to make patterns and lines. Add more color as desired.

4. Draw directly on the surface with the soft pastel and then paint over it with matte medium.

5. Add water to thin and spread the color as desired.

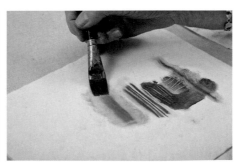

Glazing with Oil Pastels

I discovered this technique by accident. I needed to increase the contrast and color in a piece that was already finished, and I didn't want to use paint. I used the technique described below, and I loved the way I could control the contrast and color.

The coats are so thin that they don't need to be heat set unless you are working on fabric that will be washed. In that case, heat set by placing copy paper under and on top of the piece and ironing it. I know you will love the technique because of its ease and versatility on any absorbent surface.

This piece was created using white-on-white patterned fabric for the background. Washes of color were painted onto the fabric before pieces of deli paper and painted fabric were sewn to the surface. A piece of air-dry clay was sewn to the upper left-hand corner and glazes of oil pastel color were applied to selected areas.

This piece was created on Kirkland photo paper painted with acrylic washes (page 35). Three pieces of acrylic-glazed, rubber-stamped fabric were glued to the surface. An additional painted and stamped strip of fabric was glued over the middle fabric strip. The entire piece was then glazed with oil pastels to strengthen the colors and contrast.

Created on illustration board with layers of washes, resists (pages 43–64), and textures (pages 65–83), this entire piece was glazed with tones of red acrylic paint. Painted pieces of Lutradur (page 22) were glued to the surface. Oil pastel glazes were applied to strengthen the composition.

Kirkland photo paper was painted with layers of acrylic paint, and collage elements were added to the background and painted with glazes of color. Acrylic paint and paper toweling were also added to the surface. Oil pastel glazes were applied over the design to make a stronger composition.

HOW-TO

1. Run a stencil brush across an oil pastel to apply color to the brush, peeling back the paper covering from the oil pastel if needed.

2. Brush the color on a paper towel or piece of scrap cloth to smooth the oil pastel color.

3. Apply the color to the piece as desired.

4. Repeat as needed, using the same or different colors.

For this piece, the card stock background was covered with handwritten words and letters before being painted with washes of color. Collage elements were glued to the surface, rubber-stamped elements were applied, and finally oil pastel glazes were added to finish the composition.

Glazing with Paint Washes

This is a very important technique because it gives you the ability to unify designs with a wash of color. The washes of color help subdue some areas and make others more important. The less water added to the paint, the thicker the wash will become. With this technique, you can turn a work that you want to discard into a spectacular piece of fabric or paper. Use this technique on any absorbent surface.

Add metallics to the wash for a thin veil of shimmer. Experiment by mixing various colors, and if you like the washes, keep them in small, covered bottles or small takeout sauce cups with lids.

You can also use Jacquard's Dye-Na-Flow as a wash. You can use it full strength, or you can dilute it about 25% for fabric if you want the wash to go further. Dilute as much as you like for paper.

The finished effect of using washes is the same on fabric and paper, with fabric being a little bit more absorbent.

Layers of acrylic washes were painted over each other to create this piece.

Many layers of acrylic color were added to collage elements glued to card stock to unify this design and create a more dynamic finished piece.

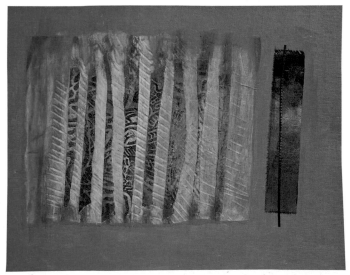

Eight strips of masking tape left over from the masking tape resist process (page 49) were glued to illustration board with Liquitex matte gel to seal the masking tape to the surface, with an additional layer of matte gel over the tape so that it wouldn't deteriorate. Layers of aqua color were applied over and around the masking tape, subduing some of the color from the tape. A collage element and piece of fabric cord (page 16) were added to the surface to finish the design.

This piece was created by using many layers of washes and scratching into the wet paint. To create highlights, paint was removed in some areas using rubbing alcohol applied to paper toweling or a soft piece of fabric (page 68).

HOW-TO

1. Squeeze acrylic paint into a dish or cup and add enough water to make the paint the consistency of skim milk. If the paint is too thick, it will cover the design that you paint over. Test the diluted paint on a discarded painted sample to make sure it is thin enough to let the design show through.

2. Apply the wash, or washes, to the piece as desired.

3. Use different colors and repeat as needed.

Inktense

Inktense products are brilliant, water-soluble colored ink pencils and blocks from Derwent. They do not have to be heat set even when used on fabric. When used with water, Inktense creates gorgeous washes of color. Fabric remains soft and it is easily sewn by hand or machine. Inktense can be used on any absorbent surface. I am so addicted to Inktense that I had to pull myself away from using it and do the other samples for the book.

Tip

You can also spray the surface to be printed, apply color to the stamp with the pencil, and then print it. The image will be a little lighter with this technique.

To stamp layers of Inktense color on illustration board, I sprayed the rubber stamp, then applied the color with the side of the pencil, and then stamped on the surface. To complete the design, I added thin lines of color with an Inktense pencil.

This piece was made using white gesso resist (page 52) on fabric, with washes made with Inktense blocks applied over the gesso when it was dry.

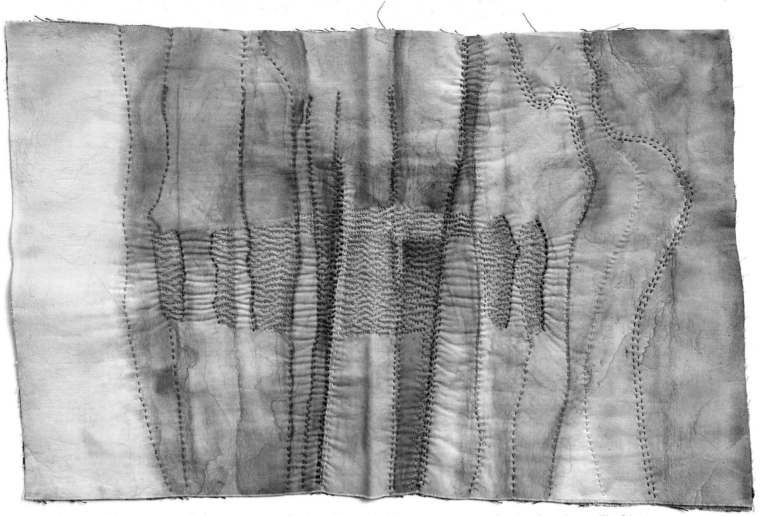

In this piece, Inktense was applied to white cotton fabric and sprayed with water to create washes in selected areas. The fabric was hand sewn to a thin piece of batting with a running stitch using variegated thread to highlight the design.

HOW-TO

1. Spray a surface with water and draw with Inktense. The color will bleed beautifully. Spray more and add more colors as desired.

2. Add more color to the wet surface.

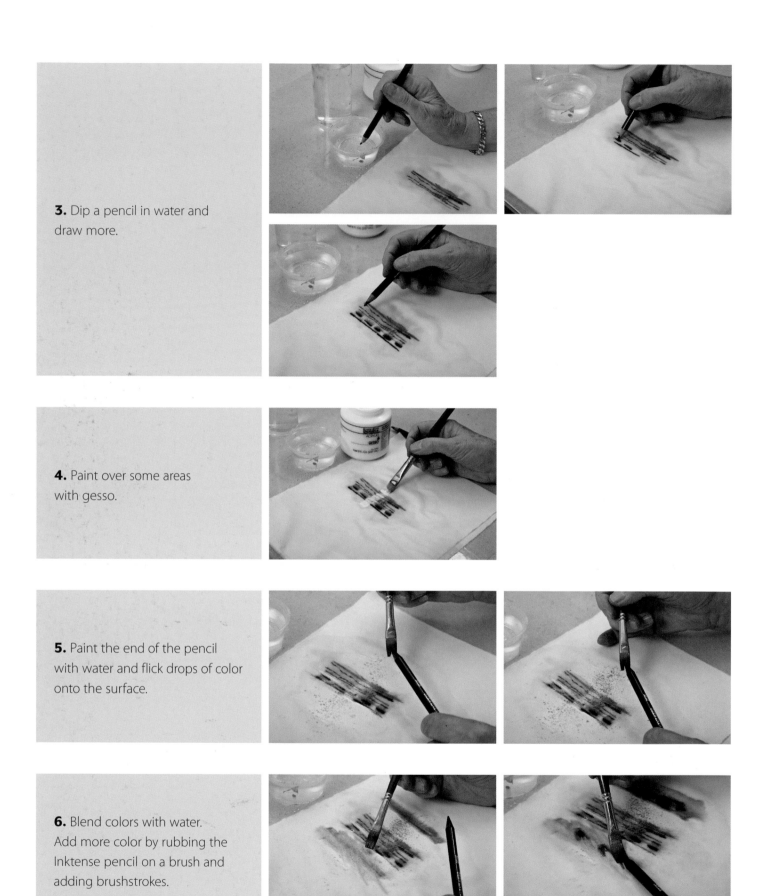

3. Dip a pencil in water and draw more.

4. Paint over some areas with gesso.

5. Paint the end of the pencil with water and flick drops of color onto the surface.

6. Blend colors with water. Add more color by rubbing the Inktense pencil on a brush and adding brushstrokes.

Water-Soluble Markers

A water-soluble marker is any marker that is water based and dilutes with water. I love working with these markers because they allow me to create interesting designs on paper and fabric. Try different papers and different fabrics for this technique. Silk is especially dramatic.

When using this technique with fabric, I usually put two or three layers of fabric on top of one another. After creating the marker design, I spray the pieces of fabric below the water-soluble marker design. I lay the marker design on top of the wet fabric and spray it, so the design also transfers to the wet fabric in all the layers.

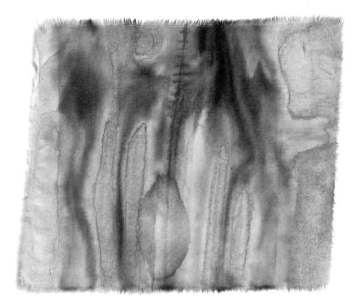 

To create these pieces, I applied layers and layers of marker color on a piece of dry white cotton fabric and then sprayed the piece, creating beautiful patterns.

 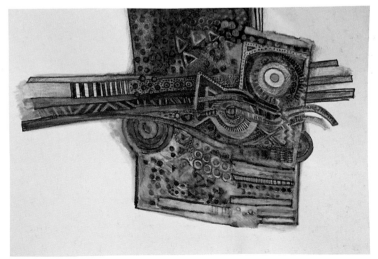

These pieces incorporate layers of water-soluble marker washes. I drew most of the design on illustration board and then added plain water washes to the marker areas with a watercolor brush to build layers of color.

HOW-TO FOR FABRIC

1. Create a design on fabric with water-soluble markers.

2. Place several pieces of water-sprayed fabric underneath. Spray a mist of water onto the design and watch the colors spread and bleed.

HOW-TO FOR PAPER

1. Draw a design on paper, card stock, or other paper product using water-soluble markers.

2. Use a detail brush and water on the design to bleed the color. Repeat as needed.

Note: The detail brush lets you control the amount of water you apply so that the design doesn't become muddy.

Resists

Crayon Resist

I think everyone has done a wax crayon resist, either in a class or in elementary school. It is fast and easy and can become fine art if done with layers and care. I think the possibilities are endless.

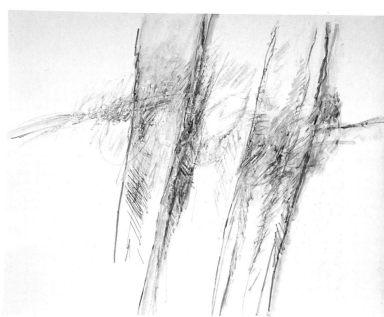

Photo paper

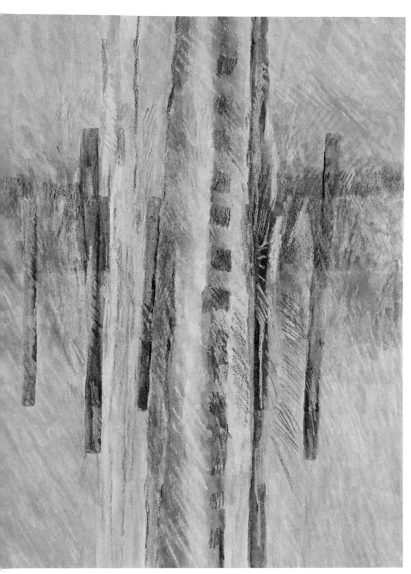

Card stock

For these samples, I drew layers of color and lines with crayons in different colors. I painted watercolor washes over the crayon layers to create complex compositions. On the photo paper sample, I applied some gesso areas to create interesting resist surfaces for paint washes.

Fabric

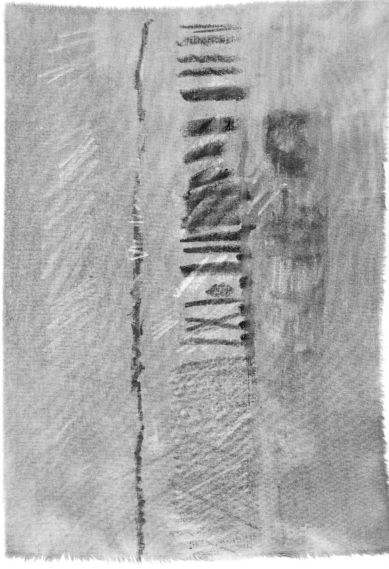

Fabric

For these samples, I drew layers of color and lines with crayons in different colors on white fabric. I painted diluted acrylic washes over the crayon layers to create complex compositions.

HOW-TO FOR FABRIC

1. Draw lines, patterns, and textures on white cotton, or any fabric of your choice. Add more pattern by rubbing the fabric with a crayon over an Impress Me rubber stamp.

2. Mist the fabric with water.

3. Apply washes of acrylic color over selected areas.

HOW-TO FOR PAPER OR CARD STOCK

1. Apply wax crayon to card stock in lines, patterns, and solid areas. Scratch into the wax if desired.

2. Mist the paper with water.

3. Apply washes of color to the crayon areas.

4. Add diluted gesso to selected areas. Blend it in with a brush or the wooden tip of a brush handle.

Gluestick Resist

With this technique you make marks with a gluestick on fabric or very thin paper and then apply washes of diluted acrylics or inks over the resist. Rubbing over rubber stamp sets makes wonderful gluestick resists. I have used my Impress Me rubber stamps, and the results are beautiful. After everything has dried, iron the piece between two pieces of copy paper.

A gluestick resist can be created as a rubbing using any textured surface, including rubbing plates, as long as the textured elements are far apart, since the glue tends to spread slightly when rubbed.

Note: Some gluesticks are very sticky. I have found that the blue and violet gluesticks work best. You can tell when the glue is dry because it turns clear, but you don't need to wait for it to dry before you proceed with painting. Be sure the gluestick is fresh and not dried out. Try different brands to see which work best for you.

Impress Me rubber stamp

Free-form gluestick marks

Impress Me rubber stamp   Colored washes applied over gluestick resists

HOW-TO

1. Place a rubber stamp face up and place a piece of fabric on top. Rub a gluestick over the fabric. The technique works best with very large, flat rubber stamps such as those from Impress Me.

2. Place 2 pieces of white fabric under the gluestick design. Spray each piece with water before applying washes of color.

3. Apply thin washes of acrylic paint over the gluestick rubbing.

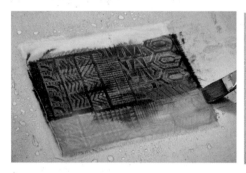

Tip
If there is still excess paint on your work surface, make a print.

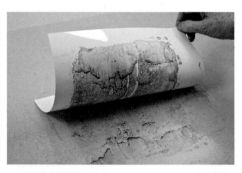

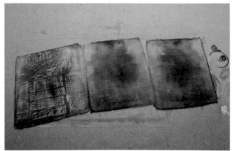

Finished, dried, and ironed pieces (including prints)

Masking Tape Resist

I've been using this technique for years, but I've continued to develop the process. I tape and then create multiple layers of color, then add more tape and then more color. I also combine rubbings (page 84) with the taping. I love the way complex surfaces can be created with this very easy technique.

Try the technique on already painted fabric or on commercial fabric to see the exciting designs that you can create.

Note: Use blue painter's tape on paper and masking tape on fabric.

Tip

You can even use the painted masking tape after you remove it. See the example in Glazing with Paint Washes (page 35).

These examples were made using tape on cotton fabric. Texture and color were added over the tape by rubber stamping (page 111), doing rubbings (page 84), applying applicator lines, applying dry sponged color, and applying washes (page 35).

This example was made using tape on cotton fabric. Texture and color were added over the tape by rubber stamping (page 111), doing rubbings (page 84), applying applicator lines, applying dry sponged color, and applying washes (page 35).

HOW-TO

1. Apply tape to the chosen surface (blue tape for paper, masking tape for fabric). Already painted surfaces are excellent for this technique.

2. You can apply color over the tape with either a sponge or brush, or as in this example, add color and texture with a rubber stamp and then sponge out the edges to blend the design.

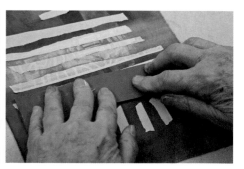

Tip

If you are applying color with a sponge, remove excess color onto another sponge or a piece of fabric or paper before applying it to the surface with the tape. Wet color will bleed under the tape onto the surface.

3. Use Twist-Up crayons and a rubber stamp to add rubbing texture. Place the rubber stamp under the dried piece and rub with the crayon on selected areas.

4. Add paint using an applicator-tipped bottle to accent the edges of the tape.

5. When all the paint is dry, remove the tape.

Finished, dried, and ironed

Gesso Resist

Gesso is a magical product that is found in art supply stores and some hobby stores. Its main purpose is to prime surfaces before painting, but it has many other uses. It comes in several weights, including Liquitex's wonderful Super Heavy Gesso.

Gesso is totally waterproof. By applying it to a wet painted surface you can produce incredible textural areas. I love using gesso on Kirkland photo paper because the wet surface, gesso, and paint create an amazing effect.

Gesso can be used in a number of ways:

✓ Applied in layers and sanded

✓ Mixed with water for wonderful washes to subdue areas of a design

✓ Mixed with paint and water for flat washes

✓ Mixed full strength with paint and used as a flat paint

✓ Used as a resist—paint gesso on a surface, let it dry, and then paint over the gesso with washes and the gesso will resist the washes

For this piece, I applied layers of gesso to Kirkland photo paper. When it was dry, I added light paint washes (page 35). I repeated the layers of gesso and washes and, at the end, added details with diluted gesso and a small detail brush.

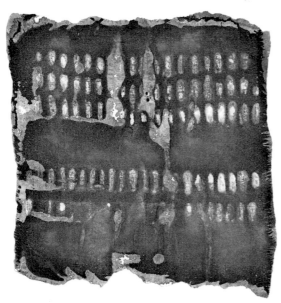

To get these effects, I applied heavy Liquitex gesso to a piece of white cotton. Then I applied washes of paint over the gesso, and they soaked through to copy paper placed below the fabric, creating the two pieces shown.

Using Kirkland photo paper, I applied gesso with a brush, and while the gesso was wet I scratched into the surface with the end of the brush handle. When the gesso was dry, I applied layers of color.

This piece was created on illustration board. I glued a variety of collage materials to the surface, including tissue paper and torn pieces from my rubber stamp catalog. I applied layers of gesso in various strengths with a brush and scratched through the wet gesso in some places. I added water to the gesso to create diluted washes that I applied over selected areas. I also added gesso to some of the paint colors. I finished the piece with some painted line work.

Using Kirkland photo paper, I applied gesso with a brush, and while the gesso was wet I scratched into the surface with the hard end of the brush handle. When the gesso was dry, I applied layers of color.

HOW-TO: USING STRAIGHT GESSO

1. Apply gesso to the chosen surface and texture it with tools of your choice, such as a nail, the end of a brush handle, or a scraping tool.

2. Apply diluted acrylic or ink washes over the gesso using an eyedropper or pipette.

3. If there is too much paint on the surface, blot or make a print.

Tip

Try painting over the gesso while it is wet and while it is dry—see how different the effects are.

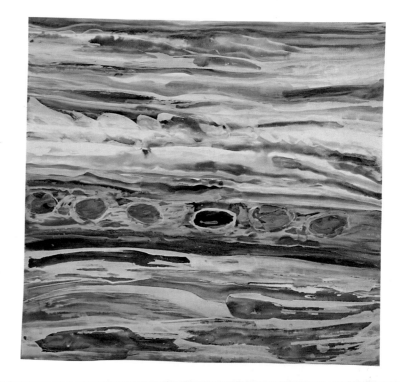

Using Kirkland photo paper, I applied gesso with a brush and then applied layers of inks and washes. The paint merged into the gesso and textured it.

HOW-TO: USING GESSO MIXED WITH WATER AND PAINT

1. Mix gesso with paint and a little water and paint onto the surface.

2. Texture the wet gesso/paint mixture.

3. Add washes of color.

Tip

Adding gesso to paint makes a flat color that is great for covering parts you want to subdue in the design.

Using Kirkland photo paper, I applied gesso with a brush and then applied layers of inks and washes. The paint merged into the gesso and textured it.

Molding / Flexible Modeling Paste Resist

Acrylic molding and modeling pastes raise the surface and act as a resist. While they are wet, you can use many different tools to create textures, which will take color differently when you apply it over the resist.

Tip

Even products such as DAP, which is used to fix grout in tub and sink areas, can be used as a resist. Only use disposable tools to texture it since it cannot be cleaned from brushes or rubber stamps. Nails work best.

This piece was created on bristol board with layers of molding paste that were applied with a credit card and scraped through a metal stencil with letters and numbers. When the paste dried, washes of color were applied to the surface.

This piece was created by applying layers of molding paste to illustration board. While the paste was wet, Impress Me rubber stamps were pressed into the surface. When the surface was dry, glazes of oil pastel color (page 32) were applied.

This piece was created on illustration board with dots created by scraping molding paste through a metal dot stencil. The rest of the molding paste was applied with a credit card and textured before it was dry. Some of the paste had rubber stamps impressed into it while it was wet. Layers of acrylic washes (page 35) were painted onto the surface, and gesso (page 52) was used to highlight selected areas.

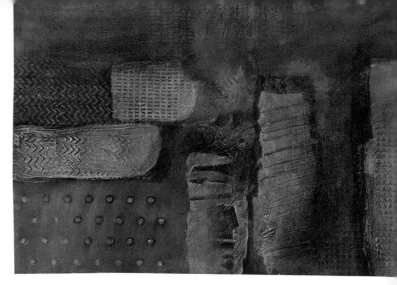

This piece was created on white cotton fabric. Molding paste was applied to the surface with a credit card, and Impress Me rubber stamps were pressed into the surface while the paste was wet. After the paste dried, multiple layers of color were applied over it. Additional acrylic colors were applied to the surface to create a cohesive design. To complete the composition, painted lines were added.

Layers of molding paste were applied to the surface of illustration board with a credit card, and rubber stamps were pressed into some of the layers. When the paste was dry, glazes of orange and red-orange acrylic paint (page 35) were applied to the surface. Oil pastel glazing (page 32) was used to create contrast in the piece.

HOW-TO

1. Apply molding paste resist to the surface with a flexible spatula or an old credit card, and texture it with a nail, takeout fork, takeout knife, or other textural tool.

2. Create additional textures by pressing a textured object, such as a rubber stamp, into the wet surface. Wash the rubber stamp immediately.

3. Use a sgrafitto tool or takeout knife to draw lines.

4. Press molding or modeling paste through a stencil.

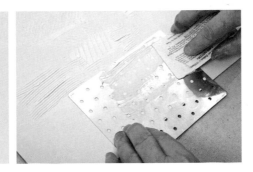

5. Let the resist dry and then apply layers of color using acrylic paint washes (page 35) or oil pastel glazes (page 32). You can also add metallic color. You can also use dry brush techniques on top of the resist to build layers of color. Try lots of ways to apply color to the resist to determine which you like best.

Petroleum Jelly (Vaseline) Resist

Petroleum jelly, such as Vaseline brand, makes a wonderful resist on fabric and paper. After creating the resist, rub an absorbent paper towel over the petroleum jelly before ironing it to remove excess petroleum jelly from the surface. On fabric, when you iron the finished resist, a thin, dark outline appears around the area where you have applied the petroleum jelly, making an interesting textural area. On paper, you can wipe away any excess petroleum jelly after the paint has dried, or you can blot the petroleum jelly with paper towels.

I applied thin layers of petroleum jelly to a plain white piece of fabric, and then scratched through the petroleum jelly to create repeat lines, leaving some of the jelly untouched. I sprayed the fabric with water and applied layers of Dye-Na-Flow and diluted acrylic paint washes. After the piece was dry, I ironed it to remove the excess petroleum jelly.

This piece was created on Kirkland photo paper. I applied petroleum jelly to a rubber stamp with a wadded paper towel and stamped the image onto the photo paper. I repeated this process nine times. I painted layers of diluted acrylic washes over the jelly. After the paint was dry I placed a paper towel on top of the rubber-stamped images. I rolled a brayer over the towel to remove the excess petroleum jelly from the surface, repeating the process until all of the petroleum jelly was removed.

I applied petroleum jelly to various rubber stamps with a sponge square and then printed them onto Kirkland photo paper. I sprayed the paper lightly with water and then applied washes of color to selected areas with a sponge. I then repeated this process to add more depth to the composition. Next, I lightly applied solid acrylic paint colors to the top left, side, and bottom to unify the composition. I allowed the colors beneath the paint to show through, creating texture on the paper. Finally, I applied the same color to the right-hand side in the same way.

HOW-TO

1. Apply petroleum jelly to selected areas of the surface with a small sponge square. Clean the sponge with soap and water to remove the jelly, or throw it away. The jelly can also be applied with a wadded paper towel.

Tip

I cut up sponges from the paint, wallpaper, and bath departments in home improvement stores to create small sponge squares.

2. Apply petroleum jelly to rubber stamps or other shapes, and press them onto the surface. I am working on 3 layers of silk habotai in this demonstration, but any fabric or paper can be used.

Note: You can apply petroleum jelly with your fingers to a rubber stamp or other textures if desired.

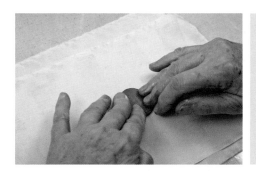

3. Spray the surface with water and apply color with a large flat brush, a pipette, a sponge square, or an eyedropper. The petroleum jelly will resist the color.

4. Make a print by placing a damp piece of fabric or a piece of card stock on the wet paint. The resulting print can be used for other creative projects.

5. When the paint is dried, wipe or blot the petroleum jelly to remove before ironing.

Finished, dried, and ironed (with prints)

Water-Soluble Wax Resist

The water-soluble wax resist technique uses a liquid wax. Painting over wax that has been applied in patterns creates diverse surfaces because the paint is resisted by the waxed areas. The wax can be applied several times to a surface. You can apply wax to patterned paper or fabric, or to any absorbent surface.

Wash wax out of brushes and tools with soap and water as soon as you are finished. See Resources (page 143) for a source for the wax.

HOW-TO

1. Apply wax to the chosen surface.

2. Scratch patterns into the wax if desired.

3. After the wax is dry, spray the surface with water and apply liquid paint.

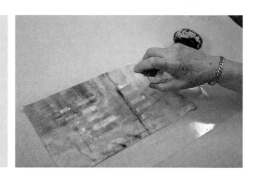

4. When the paint is dry, place the piece between deli papers or copy papers and press with a hot iron to remove the wax.

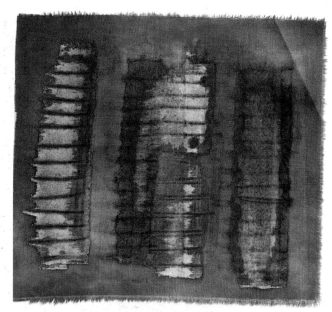

Wax resist was applied with a brush to white cotton. While the wax was wet, the hard end of a brush was used to make lines in it. Layers of acrylic washes (page 35) were applied to the dried wax.

This piece was done on white fabric. Wax patterns were applied with a brush and lines were drawn into the wet wax with the hard end of the brush. Many layers of different colors were applied with diluted acrylic washes (page 35).

White Candle Rubbing Resist

It is a lot of fun to make rubbings for resists using a white candle. Many different textures can be created by using different items such as plastic needlepoint canvas, commercial rubbing plates, metal or plastic grids of various sizes, or other stiff textured surfaces. (Rubber stamps are too soft for this technique.) Create multiple layers by adding more rubbings and paint washes. You can also use this technique over previously painted areas.

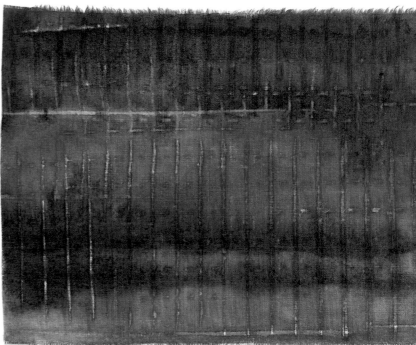

All the samples on this page were created with multiple layers of rubbings and paint washes. I let the fabric dry and ironed the pieces to remove the wax, and then repeated the process numerous times to build up a rich surface.

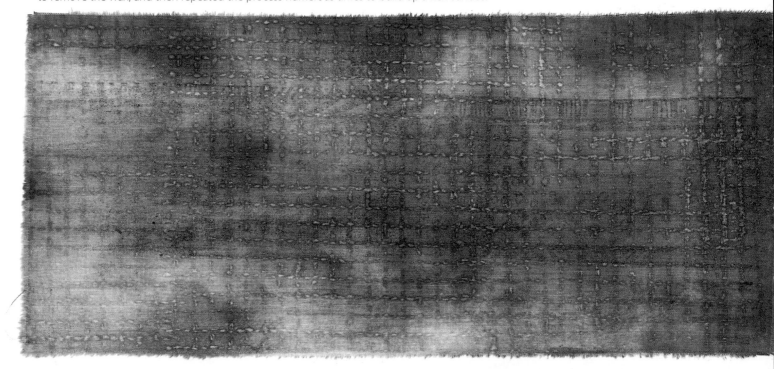

HOW-TO

1. Place a stiff rubbing plate or other hard, textured surface under thin fabric or paper. Rub very hard with the side of a candle to make sure you have left a layer of wax on the surface.

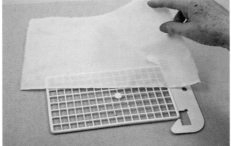 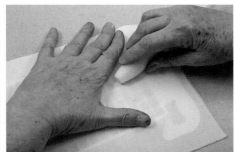

2. Wet the fabric and apply thinned acrylic paint or ink to the surface with a brush or sponge square.

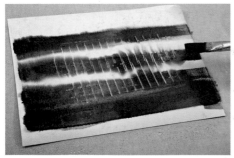  

3. Once the surface is dry, iron the piece between 2 pieces of sturdy tissue paper or copy paper to remove the wax. Repeat as desired.

Finished, dried, and ironed piece

Textures

Metal Tape

Metal tape adds a surprising element to art projects. It has an adhesive on the back and is easily cut with scissors, making it an excellent element for collage. Try scoring the metal tape with an old ballpoint pen or painting it with acrylic paints. You can find it in home improvement stores in small to large rolls.

I applied a metal tape square in the middle of a piece of square canvas board and then drew symbols on the tape with a pointed embossing tool. I applied layers of color to the tape, let them dry, and then rubbed back some of the color with a paper towel and rubbing alcohol (page 68). I added collage elements to the piece and applied layers of acrylic color (page 35) to unify the final design.

This piece was created on canvas board with strips of metal tape applied to the surface and then scored with a thin embossing tool. Layers of acrylic color were applied over the tape and surface to unify the final design.

HOW-TO

1. Cut the tape to size, remove the paper covering the adhesive, and place it on the selected area of the artwork.

2. Use an old ballpoint pen or a thin embossing tool to score the tape.

3. Apply thin layers of paint if desired.

Tip

You can wipe back the paint to reveal the metal below while it is wet, or use rubbing alcohol (page 68) when it is dry.

4. Use a wadded paper towel to spread the color.

5. Spray the paper towel with water, and wipe back and spread the color to the background.

Special Technique: Using Rubbing Alcohol

Using rubbing alcohol to remove paint from selected areas is a great way to add highlights and dimension. This technique works on acrylic paint on paper, not fabric. It also works on inkjet images on glossy paper and metal tape.

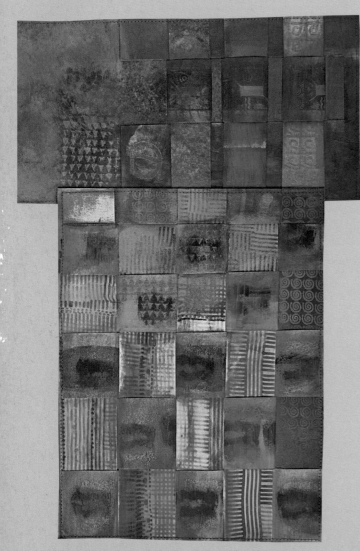

The light areas on this piece were rubbed back with alcohol to reveal the colors below.

This example shows the effects of rubbing alcohol on photo paper with black inkjet ink .

HOW-TO

1. Saturate a wadded paper towel or piece of soft fabric with rubbing alcohol.

2. Rub across areas painted with acrylic paint. The alcohol will reveal layers of color and texture.

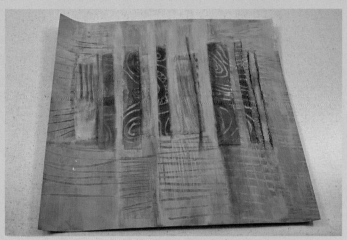

Before rubbing with alcohol

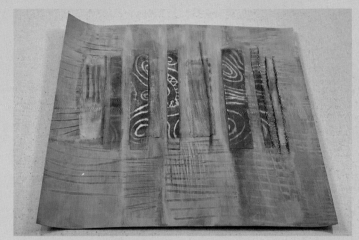

After rubbing with alcohol

Before rubbing with alcohol

After rubbing with alcohol

Paint Scraping

This is such an easy and effective technique for adding texture to surfaces. It's as simple as using the end of a wooden brush handle or a scraping tool to mark into wet paint on a surface. You can also use scrapers made specifically for artists. I use combs, takeout knives, and many other hard objects to scrape into wet paint. Try making your own scrapers with credit cards.

This piece combines a variety of collage elements, including fabric cord and painted papers and fabric. The scraped areas are clearly visible.

This example shows several layers of paint. Each layer was painted and scraped separately while wet.

After folding heavy bristol board to create these books (page 74), I applied paint to both sides, using various thick and thin acrylic layers. While the top layer of paint was wet, I scratched it to reveal the layers and colors below, repeating this process to create an interesting textured surface. I painted the pocket inserts separately, glued them to the mat board to make them stand up in the books, and placed them in the pockets after the books were constructed. Finally, I painted the back of the mat board to coordinate with the books.

This piece was created on cotton twill. I applied layers of color using wet-into-wet techniques (page 77) with acrylic washes (page 35). I scraped the wet fabric to create the lines.

This piece was created on linen fabric. I glued the major mask element to the surface and then added scraped gesso areas, rubbings on thin deli paper, rubbed collage strips, charcoal lines, and three collage elements on the bottom of the piece. The piece was raveled on the edges. It is designed to be hung unframed as a wallhanging.

This piece was created on linen fabric. For the main colored areas at the top, I glued silk colored with Inktense (page 38) to the linen. I collaged prints made with Jacquard's Dorland's Wax (page 93) on card stock on the bottom left and right. Then I added collages created with paint on deli paper to enhance the design. I added layers of acrylic paint and gesso (page 52) to the surface to complete the design. Machine sewn lines add vertical texture to the final piece.

HOW-TO

1. Mix acrylic paint with inexpensive hair gel to thicken it.

2. Apply thickened paint to the chosen surface (white, colored, or prepainted) and scrape into it with tools of your choice, such as a notched trowel, the end of a wooden brush handle, takeout knives and forks, or even your fingers.

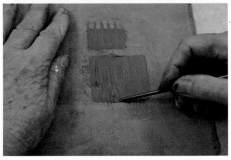 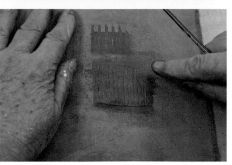

 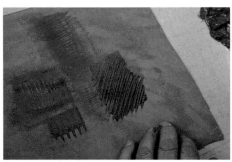

3. Add more thickened paint or additional colors and scrape again.

 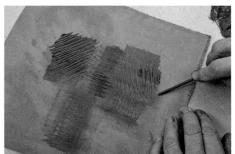

Special Technique: Making a Folded Book

Folded stand-up books are a fabulous way to showcase your art.

1. Fold a stiff piece of rectangular paper on the long side about ⅓ of the way up from the bottom. Use a bone folder or the flat end of a metal knife to crease the fold.

2. Fold the book in half across the middle, perpendicular to the first fold.

3. Make accordion folds as desired across the width of the book.

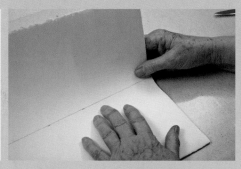 

4. Punch small holes on the 2 edges of the book to hold the folded part in place.

5. Insert small brads in the holes to hold the folds in place. Remove the brads before painting and reinsert when everything is dry.

Stenciling with Oil Pastels

I discovered this technique by accident and really love it. I use stencil brushes and oil pastels to apply color through brass and plastic stencils. The technique is easy and effective. It can be used over previously painted or collaged work to create complex effects. I have a variety of stencil brushes that fit easily in small stencil openings.

For all three samples, a stencil was placed on the chosen surface and oil pastel colors were brushed through the stencil openings with a stencil brush.

HOW-TO

1. Run a stencil brush across the oil pastel to apply color to the brush, peeling back the paper covering from the oil pastel if needed.

2. Place the stencil on the chosen surface and apply color with the stencil brush through the stencil opening.

3. Add additional color and use additional stencils as needed.

Wet into Wet

This easy technique involves applying wet paint to a wet surface. It can be used on surfaces from fabric to photo paper. Each surface will yield a different end result.

WET INTO WET ON FABRIC

This technique is very dramatic on fabric. Spray one to three layers of fabric with water and stack the layers on top of each other. Apply paint to the top layer, and the paint will seep down to the lower layers. More paint and water can be applied to the fabric, making more complex designs.

Diluted acrylic and Dye-Na-Flow washes applied in layers on silk

Diluted acrylic and Dye-Na-Flow washes applied in layers on cotton

Diluted acrylic and Dye-Na-Flow washes applied in layers on cotton

HOW-TO

1. Create diluted colors of acrylic paint in small cups or use Dye-Na-Flow right from the bottle.

2. Wet 1–3 stacked pieces of cotton or silk. Use an eyedropper, pipette, brush, or sponge to apply the first color to the wet surface.

3. Add additional colors.

4. Use a sponge to smooth the color out to the edges.

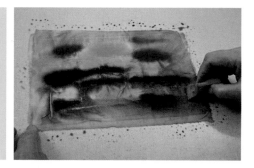

5. This technique will likely leave excess paint on your work surface. Make a print!

WET INTO WET FOR POLE WRAPPING

Another effective technique is to wrap dry fabric around a plastic or PVC pipe (from a home improvement store) and secure it with rubber bands. Spray the fabric with water. Then apply color with an eyedropper or pipette so that the paint seeps down through the fabric, making intricate designs. The size of the pole will determine the finished result. I've found that the pole wrapping technique is a lot of fun to use over already painted or dyed fabric because it increases the complexity of the finished design.

Fabric was wrapped around a PVC pipe, scrunched, and then wet with water. Different colors of diluted paint and ink were dropped onto the fabric. The fabric was allowed to dry and then unwrapped.

HOW-TO

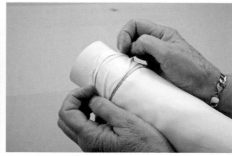

1. Wrap *dry fabric* around a plastic pole, scrunch the fabric, and hold it in place with rubber bands.

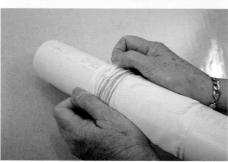

2. Saturate the fabric with water by spraying it or dipping it into a water-filled container.

3. Apply liquid colors, like Dye-Na-Flow, with a sponge square, pipette, or eyedropper.

4. When the fabric is dry, unwrap and iron it.

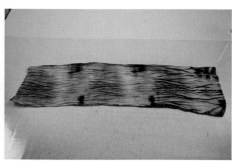

WET INTO WET ON PHOTO PAPER

I love this technique because the results are so dramatic. I use Kirkland photo paper from Costco because it doesn't buckle and the wet-into-wet patterns work well. In addition, you can print the wet paint onto another piece of photo paper, add more paint and water, and keep going. Try diluted acrylics, Dye-Na-Flow, inks, dyes, or any other thin colors for this technique.

Tip

Using the wet-into-wet technique on photo paper provides the perfect opportunity to make a print using another piece of photo paper. Printing wet paint to another slick surface generates intriguing ridges and complex paint areas.

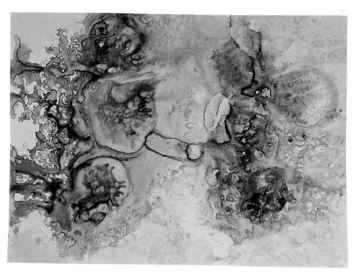

For this example, I sprayed photo paper with water before starting and applied color with an eyedropper to the wet surface. I repeated the process to achieve a fascinating surface. The bubbles were formed by pools of water and color. When the paint dried, thin lines remained around the bubbles, adding great details.

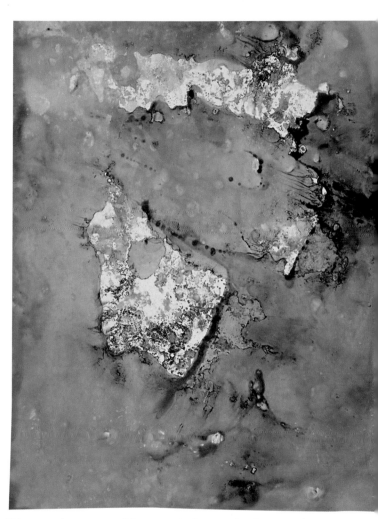

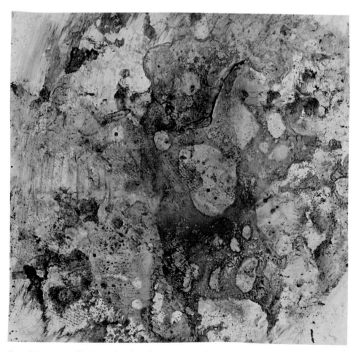

For this example, I applied color to wet photo paper and sprayed it with water so that the color moved and dripped. I didn't print the color onto another piece of photo paper, but I added additional color and sprayed again with water. I also added oil pastel glazing (page 32) to selected areas.

This example was one of those magical pieces that happened by itself. I produced about twenty pieces for this chapter in one day, printing some and not printing others. This one just worked from the moment I applied the color. It looks like an aerial view of a landscape. It was made simply by applying wet color to wet photo paper.

For this example, I applied color to wet photo paper and sprayed it with water so that the color moved and dripped. I took a print using another piece of photo paper, creating the interesting texture.

HOW-TO

1. Apply thin paint to a wet piece of photo paper, adding more water if needed.

2. Move the paint around with a paper towel.

3. Add color to fill in the background.

Tip
When the paint is dry, add additional color as needed with oil pastel glazing (page 32).

WET INTO WET WITH SALT

This is one of the easiest techniques to do. It works well on paper and on fabric. All you need is thin paint, a wet surface, and salt. The interaction of the paint and the salt makes for a tactile surface. Different salts can be used for this technique, and each will yield completely different results. Try different salts and label each one so that you will know which salt you used. Popcorn salt is especially effective.

HOW-TO

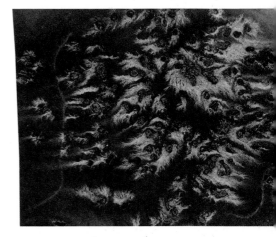

Tip

When working with fabrics, layer several pieces and the paint will seep down, creating multiple pieces.

1. Apply wet paint to a wet surface.

2. Sprinkle salt on the wet paint.

3. Let the pieces dry, separate them, and iron them to use in creative work.

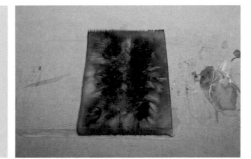

Finished, dried, and ironed

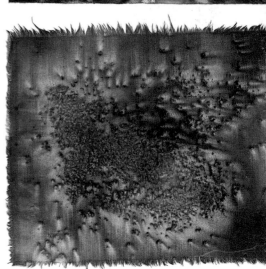

These pieces were created by applying color to wet fabric and sprinkling salt on the surface while the paint was wet. I used Jacquard Silk Salt along with Jacquard Dye-Na-Flow and diluted acrylic paints.

Rubbings

Basics

Rubbings have been around for centuries. In Great Britain, people were very busy rubbing old brasses in churches and historical spots years ago. Eventually, brass rubbing centers appeared throughout the country.

One of my fondest memories is being with my husband, Joel, in a very tiny church in a very tiny village in England doing a rubbing of a knight and his lady. We paid £2 for the privilege to a church curate. The rain poured steadily on the tin roof for the two hours that we were there. If only I could find those rubbings now.

Rubbings have taken a complete turn from the old brass rubbings. People are rubbing anything that has texture, and wonderful texture plates are available for rubbing. Rubber stamps are also excellent for rubbing. In fact, anything with texture will work as a rubbing plate—stencils, needlepoint grids, shower mats, sink mats, textured place mats, kitchen tools, and so on.

You can create your own rubbing plates by gluing textural items to foamcore board. I've used matchsticks, old watch batteries, small plastic rings, applicator sticks, plastic coffee stir sticks, and anything else I find that I can glue to the foamcore board. You will amass quite a number of your own rubbing plates. Let your imagination go wild. Use a sturdy glue to adhere the pieces to the foamcore. I use Liquitex Matte Super Heavy Gel to glue down the pieces.

MEDIA TO USE

Inktense watercolor pencils or blocks

These pencils are ideal for doing rubbings because they don't have to be heat set into fabric. They can be sprayed with water to make the colors bleed, giving a beautiful effect to the finished piece.

Permanent markers

Permanent markers tend to bleed on fabric and are a little too heavy on paper, but the rubbings created are pleasing. Use the side and the tip of the markers. Try spraying rubbing alcohol on the rubbings to get a different effect.

Rubbing on thin interfacing

I like the effect of rubbing on interfacing. The surface is a bit rough and gives a totally different look than other materials. You can create a rich surface with repeated rubbings and paint washes.

Colored pencil rubbings

Colored pencils give great detail to rubbings. Use the side of the pencil to get a smooth rubbing. If you wish to create more texture, use the point of the pencil and do a series of lines to create the rubbing. Experiment with different approaches. Use soft colored pencils for rubbings.

Twist-Up crayons

I use Twist-Up crayons from Staples. They are excellent, and a set of 24 costs about $8 online. Check crayons before purchasing them to make sure that they contain a lot of pigment and that they go on the surface smoothly.

Oil pastels

Oil pastels come in a variety of colors and intensities. Inexpensive oil pastels will usually work, but try them first to see whether they are flaky or smooth. If the oil pastel is very flaky, the result will not be satisfactory.

Tip

Be sure to try rubbing with oil pastels using stencil brushes (page 75).

Impress Me rubber stamps were placed under a piece of black fabric and rubbed with oil pastels and soft colored pencils. I created some rubbing plates and made rubbings using those plates as well. Additional color, using soft colored pencils, was applied to selected areas to boost the final composition.

Layers of Twist-Up crayons were applied to thin fabrics placed onto Impress Me rubber stamps. The pieces were sewn to a piece of colored felt. Additional collage elements were added, and paint was applied with a brush to create more dramatic areas. An embellishment (created with layers of paper glued to one another) was added to the collage and highlighted with additional paint.

Thin cottons were placed on plastic rubbing plates, including a plate with tiny dots in a repeat pattern on the surface. The rubbed fabric pieces were glued to another piece of fabric, and washes of color were applied to strengthen the composition. To finish the piece, layers of colored pencil were applied to selected areas.

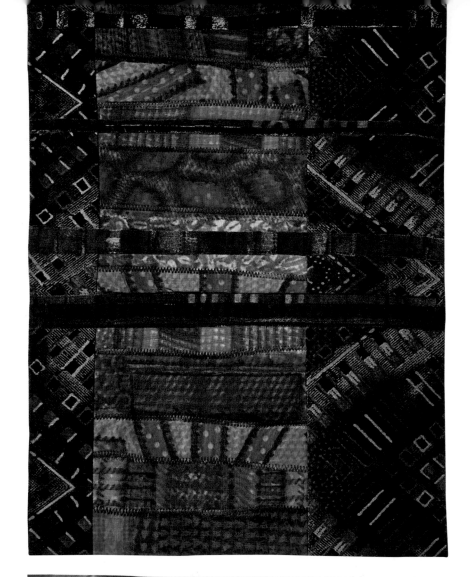

To create the rubbings in this piece, I used the side and tip of a permanent marker on plastic rubbing plates. I sewed the pieces together to form a small quilt. The side pieces are from my collection of fine fabrics from Robert Kaufman Fabrics. To complete the piece, I glued the small hanging to a piece of canvas board.

To create this piece on nonfusible thin interfacing from a fabric store, I rubbed over various rubbing plates with oil pastels and then applied layers of diluted acrylic over the rubbings. I blotted the colors while they were wet so that the rubbings would show through. To finish the piece, I applied a thin gold line across the middle with a gold oil pastel.

The central piece of this design was created by rubbing crayons across rubbing plates. I used a plastic knife to scrape most of the crayon from the surface, revealing the design below. The final composition has strips of different rubbings using oil pastels on deli paper that I ironed onto card stock, transferring and setting the designs. I collaged the deli paper rubbings to each side of the central piece and added painted blue cloth strips to complete the design.

I created this piece by rubbing over Impress Me rubber stamps with Twist-Up crayons on thin fabric. Twist-Up crayons do not leave little flakes on the surface, making them ideal for rubbings.

This piece combines various pieces of dyed silk glued to a piece of illustration board. All of the pieces were rubbed with Twist-Up crayons before they were glued to the board.

This piece includes various rubbings on fabric collaged to a piece of canvas board. I used colored pencils and some washes to coordinate the very busy composition.

This piece combines rubbings, washes, sewing elements with a running stitch, and tiny embellishments.

This piece incorporates a collage of rubbings glued onto a piece of canvas board. To finish the piece, I glued horizontally rubbed strips and a piece of thin fabric near the top of the design.

HOW-TO: BASIC RUBBING TECHNIQUE

1. Place the rubbing plate or rubber stamp face up and cover the plate or stamp with thin paper or fabric.

2. Select the medium you wish to rub with (see examples, pages 84–90). Gently rub across the fabric or paper so that the pattern from the rubbing plate appears.

Oil pastel

3. Move the fabric or paper around the rubbing plate, creating layers of colors and patterns. Feel free to use different media within a single rubbing.

Inktense pencil

Twist-Up crayon

This piece is composed of strips of different rubbings using oil pastels on deli paper. I ironed the rubbings onto card stock, transferring and setting the designs. I then collaged the deli paper rubbings to a piece of illustration board and added paint layers and details to coordinate the design.

HOW-TO: IRONING HEAVY OIL PASTEL RUBBINGS ONTO FABRIC AND PAPER

This technique is good for surfaces that are difficult to rub onto directly.

1. Make a rubbing on fabric, deli paper, or tissue paper. Use a very heavy application of color. I also suggest using dark, vibrant colors. I usually use oil pastels for this technique.

2. Place a piece of fabric or paper on top of the rubbing and press with a hot iron to transfer the rubbing. You can use fabric, but paper is better.

Printmaking

Dorland's Wax

Dorland's Wax is an amazing product, available in art supply stores. It was created for use with fine art work, but I use it in several ways. Dorland's Wax does not dry out, so it gives the artist or crafter a long time to work. Added to paint and brushed on a surface, it emulates the look of oil painting. I also love doing printmaking with it—the wax acts as a resist and allows me to create multiple layers and scratch through the layers with embossing or scraping tools. The prints are wonderfully textured. I iron the finished print between pieces of copy paper to set the wax. See the note on ironing below.

Tip

Note on ironing: Teflon ironing sheets placed on the ironing board to protect it are especially helpful in ironing waxes and other resists. I place copy paper on either side of the finished pieces and iron on the hottest setting.

To create these samples, I applied Dorland's Wax to white sheets of heavy copy paper. I scratched into the wax with embossing and scraping tools to make lines. Then I painted diluted acrylic over the wax, made a print, and repeated the process to make further prints until satisfied with the results. I ironed the pieces to heat set the wax. Additional acrylic paint was added to complete the composition.

To create these samples, I applied Dorland's Wax to white sheets of heavy copy paper. I scratched into the wax with embossing and scraping tools to make lines. Then I painted diluted acrylic over the wax, made a print, and repeated the process to make further prints until satisfied with the results. I ironed the pieces to heat set the wax. Additional acrylic paint was added to complete the composition.

HOW-TO

1. Choose plain or painted paper for this technique (fabric will work but not as well as paper).

2. Apply Dorland's Wax to the print surface with a sponge, brush, or palette knife.

3. Scratch patterns or textures into the wax.

To create these samples, I applied Dorland's Wax to white sheets of heavy copy paper. I scratched into the wax with embossing and scraping tools to make lines. Then I painted diluted acrylic over the wax, made a print, and repeated the process to make further prints until satisfied with the results. I ironed the pieces to heat set the wax. Additional acrylic paint was added to complete the composition.

4. Brush or sponge a layer of paint the consistency of cream over the wax.

5. Place paper or fabric on the print surface and press with your hands.

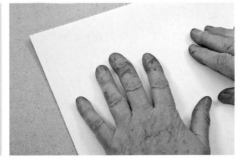

6. Lift up the print.

7. Repeat the steps as needed.

Foam Squares

This technique uses ¾″ × ¾″ square foam blocks that I found in a dollar store—they seemed ideal for making prints. This technique is very, very easy and lots of fun.

For these pieces, I scored the tops of the foam blocks with a ballpoint pen (you can make designs on all the sides and use each design as needed). Simple designs are best because the surface is so small. I made repeat prints with the design, turning it different directions and changing colors. Adding paint washes (page 35) unified and created subtlety for the final composition.

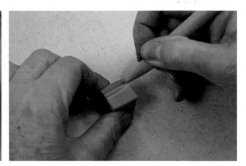

1. Score the top of the square with a ballpoint pen, embossing tool, or sharp wooden tool.

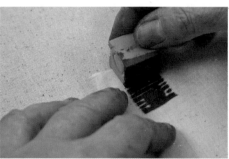

2. Pat paint on the square and print.

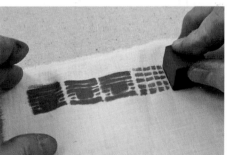

Tip

I usually squeeze paint onto one sponge square and pat it on another to spread the paint before sponging onto rubber stamps, foam squares, or other printable textures.

Fun Foam

Fun foam with a tacky back is a marvelous product for many things, but it is ideal for printing. You can create complex designs by scoring into the foam. The foam can also be cut into any shape. After creating the design and cutting the foam into the desired shape, peel the backing from the fun foam and apply the piece to a canvas board or another stiff surface for printing.

Fun foam plate that has been used for printing. You can see how complex the design turned out. I scored lines on the fun foam after adhering the pieces to canvas board. I was able to manipulate the cut-out fun foam into complex shapes.

For these pieces, I placed card stock on top of the fun foam plate covered with paint and used a brayer and my hands to create the print. I made multiple, overlapping prints to make complex designs. Adding soft colored pencil details in selected areas made the prints more dramatic.

This piece was created on cotton fabric with layers of acrylic washes (page 35) painted on the fabric. Fun foam prints were repeated across the fabric, and to finish the piece, additional paint details were added with a detail brush. Colored pencil layers enhanced the final composition.

A card stock background was painted with a neutral color of acrylic paint. Multiple prints were applied in overlapping patterns to the surface, resulting in a complex pattern.

HOW-TO

1. Cut and glue pieces of fun foam to a canvas board. Draw lines on the fun foam with a ball-point pen or sharp wooden tool.

2. Sponge color onto the design and print with it on the selected surface. Repeat as desired, building up layers of color and patterns.

3. Add washes of color (page 35) to unify the design.

Tip

Misting the print plate can provide better printed images.

Gelli Plates

I learned how to use gelatin to make printed images from Rayna Gillman's book *Create Your Own Hand-Printed Cloth*. I was so obsessed with the technique that I hardly ate or slept for about a week. (My husband, Joel, was gone for that period of time.) Now there is a great product on the market called Gelli Plate that is permanent and reusable (see Resources, page 143). Using Gelli Plates is the same as making monoprints (page 103) and is very easy.

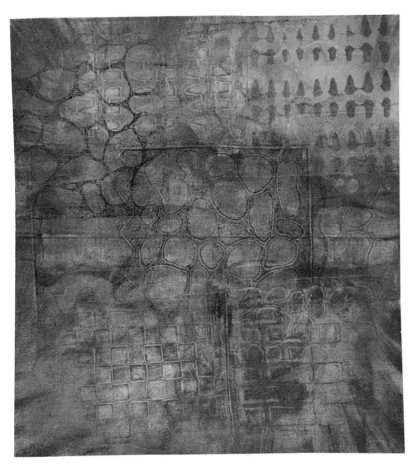

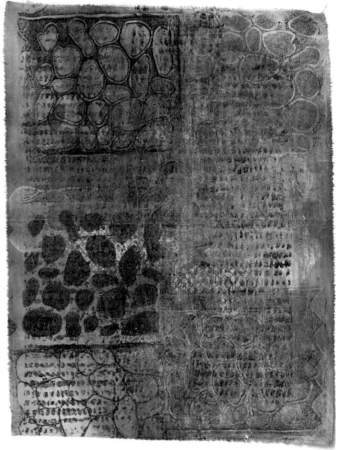

These pieces were created on prepainted fabric. I patted paint onto the Gelli Plate and pressed a stencil into the paint. I printed from the Gelli Plate and also printed the stencil, changed colors, and repeated the process, creating the complex designs.

Important! Do not use photo paper with the Gelli Plate. Photo paper sticks to the plate and won't come off. Only use other types of paper or fabric for this technique. The first print I did with the Gelli Plate was on Kirkland photo paper; it took me an hour to peel the paper from the plate, and it left little pits in the surface.

HOW-TO

1. Apply paint to the Gelli Plate. (I use a sponge square to apply the paint to the surface. Smooth sponges work best.)

2. Place a stencil, rubber stamp, leaves, sequin waste, or any other textured pattern on the wet surface. Press.

 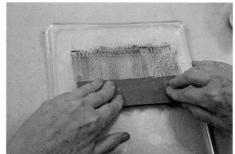

3. Remove the textured item, and place fabric or paper onto the painted, textured Gelli Plate; press firmly with your fingers on the back of the surface. Be sure to press on every part of the surface so that the entire design prints.

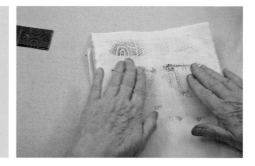

4. Pull the print and repeat Steps 1–3, using different colors and textures if desired.

Tip

After using an item to create texture on the Gelli Plate, give it a mist with water and use it as a stamp to make another print.

Monoprints

Monoprint designs can be simple or very complex. Monoprints are easy to make, and the technique has been around for hundreds of years. The process involves applying paint to a slick surface such as freezer paper, glass, or smooth plastic and then making a print from the wet paint. This is the same process used with Gelli Plates (page 101). I add inexpensive hair gel to the paint to lubricate it and make it slick for printing. You can create prints on top of prints to add as much complexity as you like.

Using a plastic print plate, I added hair gel to paint, applied it to the surface, and scratched into the wet surface with a scraping tool to make the design. I made the print on fabric and then finished the piece with washes of color (page 35) around the print.

For this piece, I sponged color plus hair gel on a piece of freezer paper and laid a piece of photo paper on top of the paint. I flipped the print so that the freezer paper was on top and rubbed the back vigorously with my fingers to make the print. When I removed the freezer paper, little ridges of color were created on the surface.

I applied hair gel to a piece of freezer paper with sponge squares and a rubber stamp. I sprayed the surface with water while the hair gel was wet and applied thin colored washes to the surface with an eye dropper. While the paint and hair gel was wet, I made a print with habotai silk. Colored washes were added to unify the design.

HOW-TO

1. Apply paint to a slick surface such as freezer paper, glass, or plastic. You can use a brush or sponge.

2. Press objects onto the wet surface and pull them off immediately, or use a blunt-ended tool to score the painted surface.

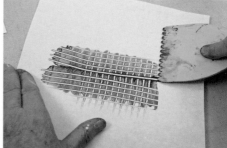

3. Press a piece of fabric or paper onto the painted surface and use a brayer or your hands to transfer the paint to the fabric or paper.

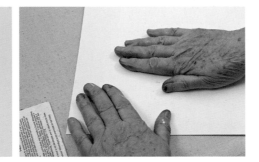

4. Remove the paper or fabric to reveal the design (see the print on the right side of the photograph).

5. Repeat as desired to build up a complex design.

6. Scrape wet paint with a credit card.

7. Place the design on the fabric and rub the back of freezer paper.

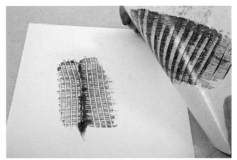

8. Reveal the design.

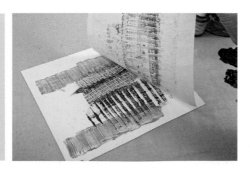

Inktense Monoprints

I've tried using Inktense products in as many ways as possible. I discovered that Inktense is easy to use for monoprinting, and you can overlap prints for a more complex surface.

Tip

To make a monoprint plate, I bought a thin piece of plastic and had it sandblasted to create a roughened surface that would accept the Inktense pencils.

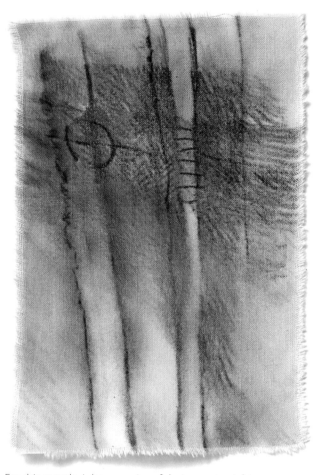

For this sample, I drew a series of designs using Inktense pencils on a monoprint plate (page 103). I sprayed the design with water, placed fabric on top of the wet design, and pressed with my fingers on the back of the fabric to make a print. I repeated the process to make a more complex design. To create solid colors, I sprayed the fabric with water and painted washes using Inktense blocks.

For this sample, I reused the plate from the piece at left. I sprayed the design with water and made two prints on card stock. When monoprinting with Inktense and water, always check after you pull your first print—you may be able to get more prints!

1. Draw a design on a piece of white fabric, card stock, or a monoprint plate (page 103).

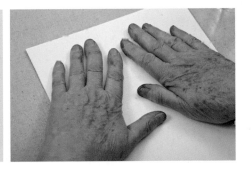

2. Spray the design with water and place a piece of fabric or paper on top.

3. Rub to transfer the design.

4. Remove the print.

Rubber Bands

I have been using this technique for a while, but I have gone further with it recently, making more complex prints and using different sizes of rubber bands. This is another very easy and fun technique. Use it on plain fabric or paper, or for a different and more complex look, use it on already painted surfaces or commercial fabrics or papers.

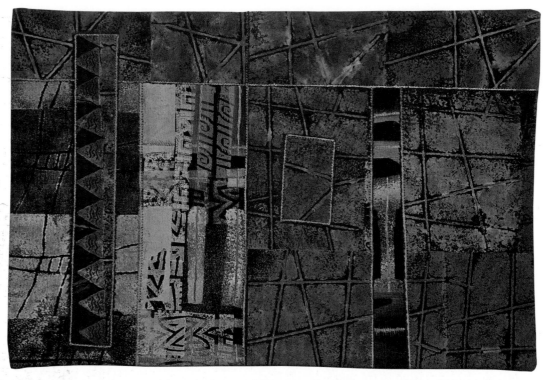

This piece is a fabric collage of various images from rubber bands and rubber stamps. I used raw-edge appliqué to include layers and layers of printed designs in the final piece.

For this print I used very wide rubber bands on black fabric. To get the repeat of the chevron design at the center bottom of the print, I blocked the lower area of the design with copy paper. I printed the top of the rubber band plate and then covered it with paper, made another print, and so on to make the repeat pattern. The rest of the design was straight printing with the rubber band plate.

These prints started with white fabric. I patted paint onto the rubber band print plate and made the prints. While the prints were wet, I flipped them over and sponged Dye-Na-Flow on the backs of the pieces. The Dye-Na-Flow bled onto any open areas of the fabric, making a vibrant final design.

This design was made by doing a rubber band print on a previously painted piece of fabric. I added paint washes to make a more dramatic final design.

HOW-TO

1. Cut a piece of stiff cardboard to the desired size.

Note: I also use small canvas and foamcore boards for rubber band printing.

2. Stretch individual rubber bands in different directions on the stiff board until you are satisfied with the pattern. You can overlap the rubber bands when creating the effect you want.

3. Pat paint with a sponge onto the rubber band print plate.

4. If you are using fabric, place it on top of the painted rubber bands and press with your fingers on the rubber bands and the spaces in between them. If you are using paper, only the rubber bands will print. It is hard to press stiff paper into the spaces between the rubber bands. You can use softer paper, such as rice paper, and it will act like fabric.

5. Lift off the paper or fabric and repeat Steps 3 and 4 as desired, changing colors or the patterns of the rubber bands.

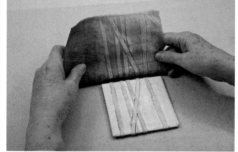

Rubber Stamps

In 1996 my husband and I started a rubber stamp company called Impress Me. From the beginning, people seemed to like the unusual stamp images that I drew by hand. In April 2010 we discontinued our old stamps and now make only unmounted stamps that are approximately 8″ × 10″. These stamps can be used for rubbings, stamping, and all forms of printing. The samples in this section were made with our new stamps and show the possibilities of using rubber stamps in your designs. Note that I have used different surfaces for the techniques shown.

This piece was created on Kirkland photo paper. I printed the rubber stamp images on the paper with acrylic paint and then used acrylic washes (page 35) to complete the design.

This piece was created on pieces of prepainted fabric. I patted acrylic paint color on one section of the stamp, applied a different color beside it, and repeated the process across the stamp. I lightly misted the acrylic paint and then placed the painted fabric on top of the stamp. I rubbed vigorously with my fingers on the back of the fabric.

I made a series of prints on white fabric by patting white acrylic paint onto a stamp set and printing the designs. I added paint washes (page 35) over the prints to strengthen the designs.

This print was made on interfacing with acrylic paint. After the paint dried, I applied washes of diluted acrylic to the design.

This piece is a collage of various rubber stamp prints. I sewed the pieces to felt and then sewed layers of rubber-stamped images to the surface. I repeated three small orange rectangles on the left side of the design to make a stronger composition.

Tips

· I add inexpensive hair gel to my acrylic paint (about 60% gel, 40% paint) to make it slick so that it prints well. It also helps the paint wash off the rubber stamp easily.

· After creating the rubber-stamped image, wash the rubber stamp immediately with a rotary toothbrush and water.

· If paint dries on the rubber stamp, use rubbing alcohol and a stiff brush to clean it.

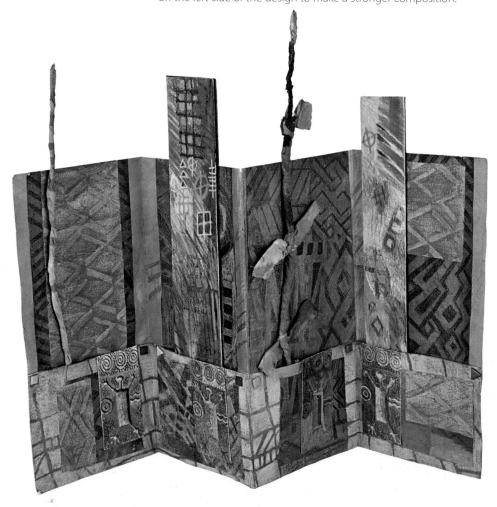

This folded book (page 74) shows rubber stamping to intensify the finished results. I collaged layers on the book elements and strengthened the rubber-stamped images with colored pencils. I made the flags out of fabric cord (page 16). The right-hand flag has painted fabric strips tied to it. The stiff pieces of cardboard feature stamping, layers of paint, and colored pencil.

HOW-TO

1. Place the rubber stamp face up and pat paint on it with a sponge square.

2. Place fabric or paper on top of the rubber stamp and press firmly with your fingers or a brayer to make the print.

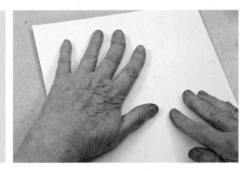

3. Lift up the paper or fabric to reveal the print.

4. After you've made a print, spraying a mist of water on the remaining paint on the stamp may allow you to make another, lighter print or two.

5. Repeat as desired with multiple images of the same stamp, or with different stamps and different colors. Add washes of color (page 35) to unify the design.

Tip

You can also print on commercial or prepainted surfaces, creating more complex designs.

Paint + Hair Gel Stamped on Photo Paper

This technique is especially effective on photo paper. I use Kirkland photo paper for many of my projects. It is an excellent surface for collage because it doesn't buckle and it accepts paint and other media. It comes in different sizes at the store, but I use the 8½″ × 11″ size. It is available online as well, in 11″ × 14″ and 16″ × 20″ sheets, from www.costco.com.

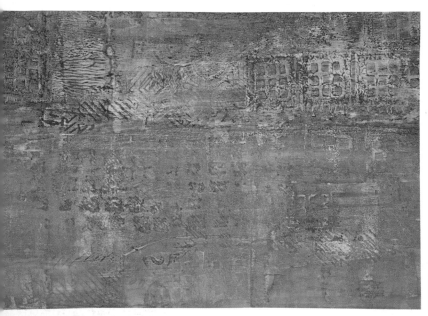

I mixed acrylic paint in a 50/50 mixture with inexpensive hair gel and patted various color mixtures onto the photo paper. I pressed different stamp patterns into the wet paint and added paint glazes over the designs. I repeated the process, producing complex finished compositions.

HOW-TO

1. Sponge paint combined with hair gel onto photo paper.

2. Press a rubber stamp into the wet paint and remove.

Tip

Mix the hair gel and paint in an approximately 40% paint / 60% hair gel ratio. Use more hair gel with very thick paint. As you use the hair gel and paint combination, you will discover the best ratio of paint and hair gel for your creative pieces.

3. Repeat as needed to complete the design.

Tip

For a different look, use different colors of paint with one stamp.

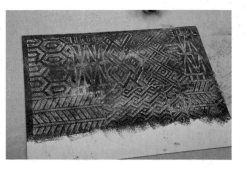

Silkscreens

I love to silkscreen because it doesn't have to be compli-cated. This chapter includes using white glue and masking tape as resists on the back of a blank silkscreen.

This is the first print of glue on the back of a silkscreen.

These four prints show the glue breaking down. On the last print, I added colored pencil to enhance the design.

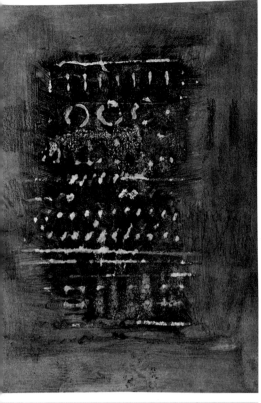

HOW-TO: USING GLUE ON THE SILKSCREEN

1. Apply water-soluble glue, such as Elmer's School Glue, to the *back* of a blank silkscreen and let it dry thoroughly.

2. Mix acrylic paint with hair gel in a 60% gel, 40% paint combination.

3. Place a piece of paper or fabric on the work surface under the silkscreen.

4. Place paint/gel at the top of the screen and use a credit card, squeegee, or plastic scraper to scrape the color through the screen onto the paper or fabric. Use firm pressure and scrape the paint at a 45° angle.

5. Carefully lift the screen to see the result.

6. Repeat Steps 2–5 as desired using a different color of paint. The glue will start to decompose as you do successive screenings, which in itself can produce interesting effects.

Tip

If there is too much paint on your screened image, make a print!

As an extra bonus, you also can make a print off the back of the silkscreen. If you aren't getting much of an image—or to get an additional print—try misting the silkscreen with a little water.

Created with masking tape on the back of a silkscreen

HOW-TO: USING TAPE ON THE SILKSCREEN

Placing tape on the back of a silkscreen is one of the easiest ways to create striking images.

1. Place pieces of tape on the back of a blank silkscreen.

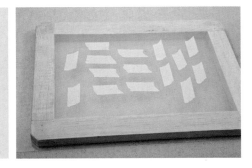

2. Follow Steps 2–5 for Using Glue on the Silkscreen (page 117).

3. Remove the pieces of tape from the silkscreen and print them onto a piece of fabric.

4. Place a piece of fabric or paper on the silkscreen and take a print from the paint remaining on the screen.

Making a print from masking tape resist on fabric

This example was created with tape on a silkscreen. It is on fabric and has oil pastel glazing (page 32) over Impress Me rubber stamps throughout the design.

Thermofax

Thermofax printing techniques have swept the craft and art world. Someone discovered that the old Thermofax machines (typically used in schools more than 25 years ago) could be used to create amazing prints. The late Jean Ray Laury was the first to introduce me to Thermofax screen printing. She created wonderful prints that she used in her quilts.

If you are lucky, you might find an old Thermofax machine in a cupboard of a school storage facility. That is what happened to me. I taught at Palisades High School in Pacific Palisades, California, for 27 years and took a chance that they might still have the old Thermofax machine that the faculty used for handouts for the students. They did have it and gave it to me. I am able to make screens to use for my creative projects.

Unlike with silkscreens (pages 116–120), where you can create a resist on the screen with glue and tape, the Thermofax screen needs the Thermofax machine to create an image. You create your design on plain paper with a carbon-based implement (such as soft pencils, black crayons, or some India inks) or simply photocopy your design (the toner in the photocopy is carbon based). The carbon tells the Thermofax machine

(a thermal copier) where to create heat, melting the screen's plastic in those areas to create your image.

Welsh Products (see Resources, page 143) has the screen material and the machines. If you don't have a machine or don't want to incur the expense of buying one, you can search the Internet for someone to create your design on a screen. You can also buy Thermofax screens with the designs already created online.

Meinke Toy is another source. The company has screens a bit heavier than Thermofax screens, and you can buy some of my designs on screens there.

Provo Craft has a machine called Yudu (see Resources, page 143). The company also sells blank screens on which you can create your own Thermofax designs.

Thermofax screens can be used alone or under a blank silkscreen. Thermofax screens are flexible. The frame of the silkscreen helps hold the Thermofax screen in place.

Note: Always clean your silkscreens and Thermofax screens immediately after using them. Dried paint is difficult and sometimes impossible to remove.

This sample is on fabric. A wash of violet was applied to the entire piece. Then successive layers of Thermofax printing were applied in various colors over the dried violet paint on the fabric. The white was applied both over and under the other Thermofax prints.

This is a Thermofax design printed onto a piece of copy paper. Additional color was added with paint washes and colored pencil. A few areas have oil pastel to make the color more vibrant.

All of these samples were created by combining prints made directly with the Thermofax screen and also by putting the screens under a silk-screen. Each piece was finished by adding paint washes. Some colored pencil was added to enrich the final composition.

This is a large piece done on bristol board. It includes sponged color washes, colored pencil, and a variety of Thermofax prints added to create a more complex finished piece. Some of the Thermofax prints were subdued with acrylic washes.

This sample was created on a large piece of bristol board. The basic painting was created with layers of color applied with a sponge. Acrylic washes were applied to subdue some of the areas. Areas of Thermofax printing were added over the painted areas. Some of those prints were subdued with additional acrylic washes. Some of the wet paint was scratched with the hard end of a brush.

HOW TO: USING A THERMOFAX SCREEN

1. Prepare your screen or purchase a prepared screen.

2. Place the prepared Thermofax screen, textured side up, on top of your fabric or paper.

3. Prepare paint to the consistency of thick cream, thinning the paint with hair gel if needed.

4. Use a spoon to put some paint on the screen and use an old credit card or paint scraper to pull the paint through the open areas of the screen, as you would for silkscreening (page 116)

5. Repeat as needed.

Note: You must clean the screen immediately after use or the paint will dry in the screen and you won't be able to use it again and again. I keep a large flat tray with water in it next to my printing area and immediately place the screen with ink in the tray. I also use the hair gel / acrylic paint combination when making Thermofax prints.

Using Inktense Pencils

Draw over the open areas on the screen with Inktense pencils. Use inexpensive hair gel to scrape through the screen where you have applied Inktense color on paper or fabric. You get a wonderful print.

Note: *You can also use a damp sponge to push the Inktense color through the Thermofax screen.*

HOW-TO: USING A THERMOFAX UNDER THE SILKSCREEN

Note: *You must have the Thermofax screen before starting this process.*

1. Place a piece of fabric or paper on your work surface and then place a Thermofax screen on top of the fabric or paper, under a blank silkscreen.

2. Follow Steps 2–5 for Using Glue on the Silkscreen (page 117).

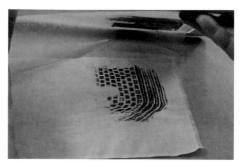

Tip

You can squeegee paint through a Thermofax screen directly, but the silkscreen keeps the Thermofax screen firmly in place, allowing for larger prints and more control of the paint as it is squeegeed onto the chosen surface.

For these samples, I placed a Thermofax screen under a silkscreen. I mixed acrylic paint and inexpensive hair gel in a 50/50 mixture. I squeegeed various colors of paint and hair gel through the silkscreen with pressure heavy enough to force the paint through the silkscreen and the Thermofax screen. I added paint washes and details to each sample. I also used colored pencils over selected areas to enhance the design.

Styrofoam Plates

This is another technique I have used before, but this time I have really pushed the possibilities. You could create using just Styrofoam prints for the rest of your time as an artist and not repeat yourself: Change the designs, overprint previous prints, try new colors, create fabric paper (page 10), collage pieces to canvas, and think of more and more ways to use the prints.

These samples were made using my Robert Kaufman fabric. I used opaque paint on the Styrofoam print plate and printed onto the fabric. I changed colors and repeated the process. The end result was a very complex piece of fabric.

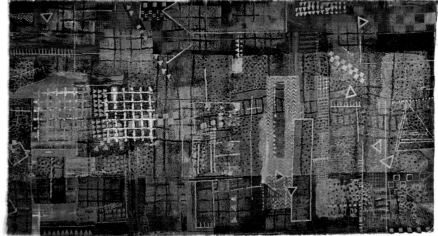

This print design was created on already painted silk. The background colors of the silk show through the prints made with Jacquard's Lumiere gold paint.

For this technique, use Styrofoam plates, meat trays, or cups. Try heavy Styrofoam and lightweight Styrofoam. Each type of Styrofoam has its own qualities. Experiment and see which produces the print you like best. I love this technique because it is so easy and everyone can produce beautiful results.

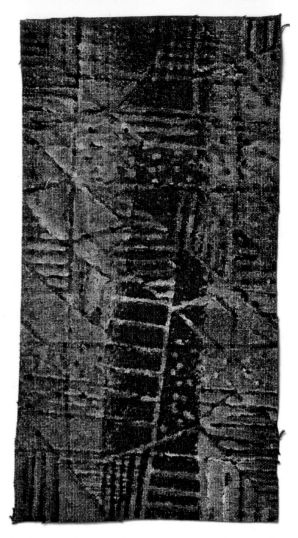

This is an example of a thin Styrofoam print plate with the color on it. It could be an embellishment for a project. Another possibility is to frame it with a painted or printed background in a shadow box for a contemporary look.

For this sample, I patted opaque paint onto the print plate and made two separate prints on black fabric. I over-lapped the prints to make a more complex finished print.

This piece was produced on black paper. I printed three different print plates using opaque paint. I trimmed the prints and glued them to a stiff piece of card stock to create the finished design.

HOW-TO

1. Cut a piece of Styrofoam to the desired size. Try triangles; long, skinny pieces; circles; squares; rectangles; and odd shapes. Try cutting out insect or animal shapes. Cut holes with a craft knife. Be experimental.

2. Draw a design with a ballpoint pen on the Styrofoam.

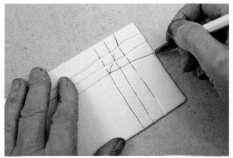 

Tip
Another way to work is to glue multiple small pieces of Styrofoam to small canvas boards for more permanent plates.

3. Pat paint onto the Styrofoam with a sponge square.

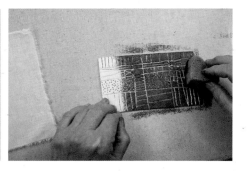

4. Place a piece of fabric or paper on the painted design. Press firmly with your fingers on the back of the paper or fabric, or use a brayer.

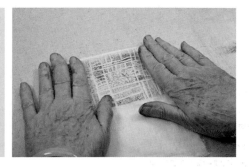

5. Remove the fabric or paper.

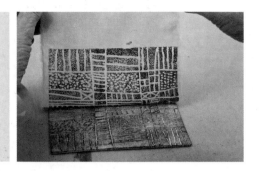

6. Repeat Steps 1–5 as desired, repeating the design, changing colors, or using different designs. You can also mist the piece with water and add a color wash to unify the design.

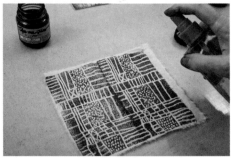

Finished, dried, and ironed

Tip

Try this technique using Inktense pencils (page 38). Apply the color to the Styrofoam, mist with water, and print. The colors will be beautifully vibrant.

Wallboard Grid Tape

In home improvement stores you can purchase rolls of very thin adhesive-backed plastic grid used for securing wallboard. The grid I used was yellow, but when teaching in Australia I found that the grids were white. The grid can be easily cut into pieces and applied to a sturdy cardboard surface, creating a print plate. Create depth by making successive layers of grid prints.

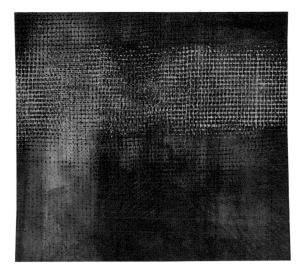

I patted acrylic paint onto a grid print plate and printed on already painted card stock. I made additional prints with other colors.

I patted acrylic paint onto a grid print plate and printed on black fabric. I made a series of prints, overlapping them and using different colors.

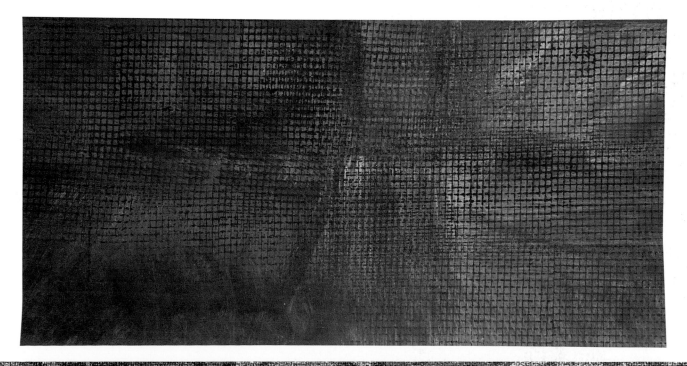

HOW-TO

1. Apply the grid to a sturdy cardboard surface, creating a print plate.

2. Use a sponge to pat paint onto the grid print plate.

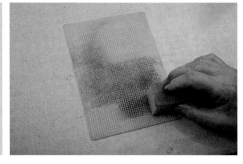

3. Make the print by turning the plate onto the chosen surface, or place the surface on top of the grid and use a brayer or your fingers to make the print.

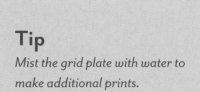

Tip
Mist the grid plate with water to make additional prints.

4. Repeat as desired to build up color and texture.

Putting It All
Together

People often ask me how I work.

The following two pages are designed to give you a quick look at making a piece from start to finish. In reality there are more steps in between—trying out different ideas (*asking "what if?"*), adding and taking away or painting over things that aren't working (*working in layers*), and of course, *making a print* when there is too much paint on the surface.

To give you even more ideas, pages 134–142 offer a gallery of finished pieces with notes that indicate the techniques used so you can refer back to those sections in the book and read about each specific technique.

FOLLOW THESE STEPS:

Glue down painted paper →

Add cheesecloth → **Paint cheesecloth** →

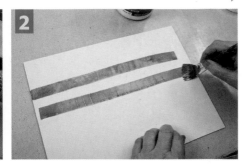

→ **Take a print** → **Add modeling paste dots** →

Add a purple wash → **Add painted Lutradur** →

Add a coating of matte medium | **Add painted paper** → | **Scrape with brush handle** →

Add gesso ⟶

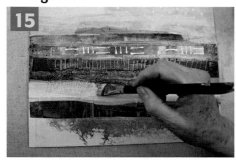

Add paint details ⟶

Paint over blue with purple ⟶

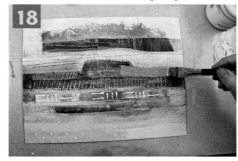

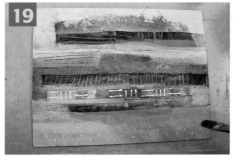

Wipe to blend ⟶

Paint with blue and gesso ⟶

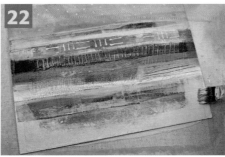

Tone down with water ⟶

Add details with a brush ⟶

Add blue paint and gesso ⟶

Add white ⟶

Darken blue ⟶

Add fabric cord ⟶

Done!

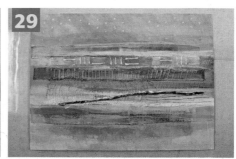

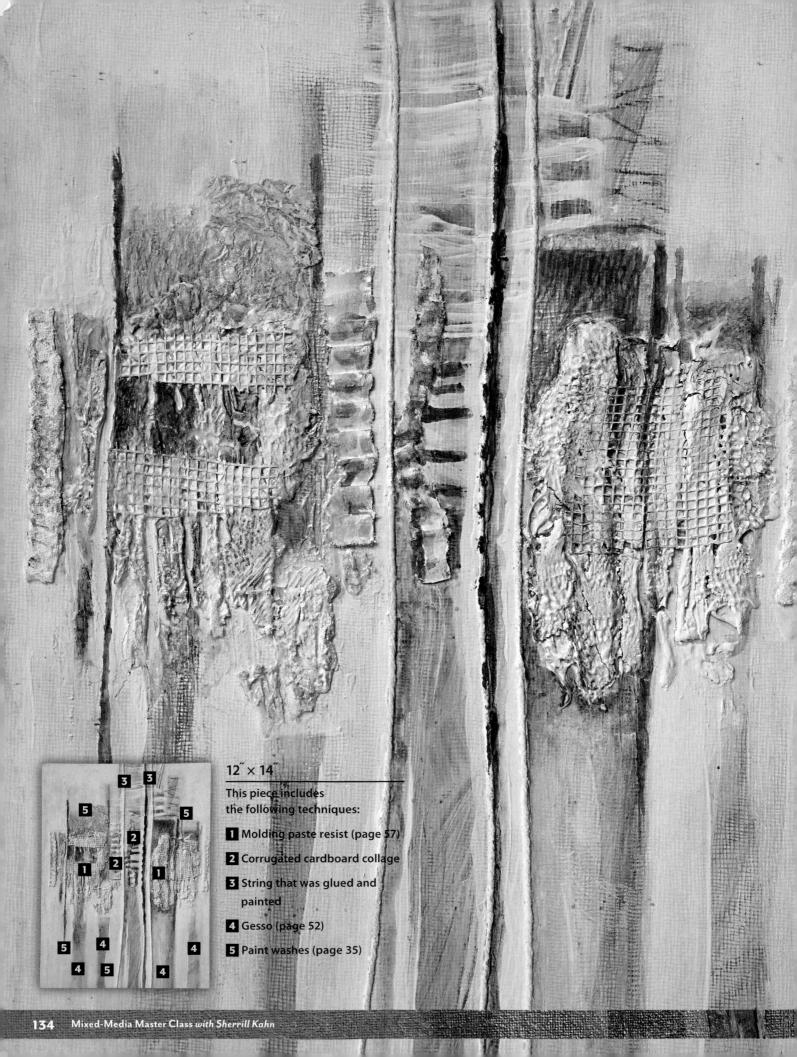

12″ × 14″

This piece includes
the following techniques:

1 Molding paste resist (page 57)

2 Corrugated cardboard collage

3 String that was glued and
    painted

4 Gesso (page 52)

5 Paint washes (page 35)

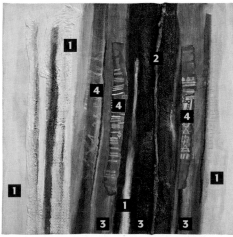

14″ × 14″

This piece includes
the following techniques:

1 Textural collage with gesso
(page 52)

2 A painted twig

3 Washes of acrylic color
(page 35)

4 Painted acrylic details

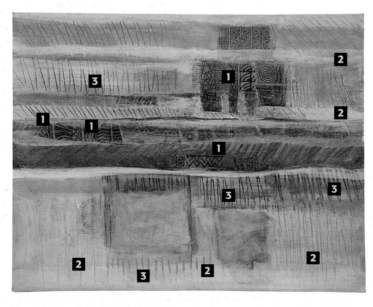

11˝ × 14˝

This piece includes
the following techniques:

1 Collage of rubber-
stamped images (page
111) from my Impress
Me rubber stamp
catalog

2 Gesso layers (page 52)

3 Lines scratched into the
wet surface

4 Glazes of acrylic color
(page 35) across whole
piece

18″ × 24″

This piece includes
the following techniques:

1 Painted Lutradur collage
   (page 22)

2 Rubber stamping (page 111)

3 Glazing techniques (page 35)
   across whole piece

4 Gesso washes (page 52)

5 Glued textural pieces

11″ × 14″

This piece includes
the following techniques:

1 Wet-into-wet techniques (page 77)
across whole background

2 Water-soluble marker washes (page 41)
across whole background and stripes

3 Ribbon appliqué

4 Scratched lines (page 70)

5 Rubbing techniques (page 84)

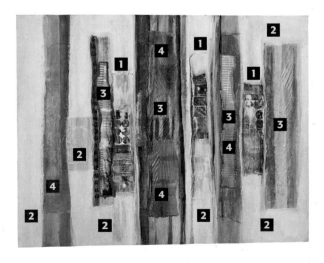

11″ × 14″

This piece includes
the following techniques:

1 Digital image collages

2 Gesso washes (page 52)

3 Painted gesso with lines
created in the wet paint with
the hard end of the brush

4 Acrylic glazes (page 35)

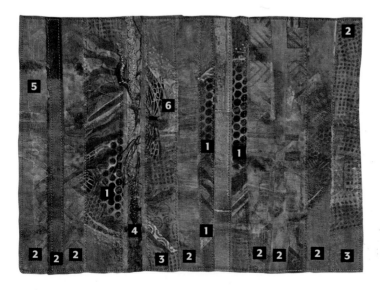

9″ × 12″

This piece includes
the following techniques:

1 Stenciling through sequin
waste (page 75)

2 Collage of strips of fabric

3 Rubber stamping (page 111)

4 Textured yarn

5 Glazes of acrylic color
(page 35) across whole piece

6 Stenciling (butterfly)
(page 75)

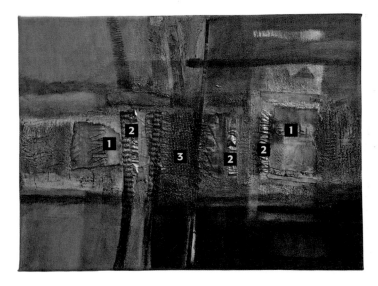

9″ × 12″

This piece includes
the following techniques:

1 Textured paper collage

2 Textured metal (page 65)

3 Plastic grid

4 Layers of glazing (page 35)
across whole piece

5 Thick and thin acrylic
washes (page 35) across
whole piece

This piece includes seven separate paintings stapled together to create the finished whole. The staples are covered with painted strips.

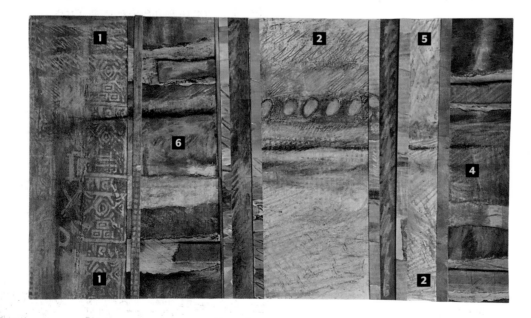

12″ × 16″

This piece includes
the following techniques:

1 Thermofax printing (page 121)

2 Scratching into wet paint
(page 70)

3 Paint glazing (page35) across
whole piece

4 Colored pencil marks (page 38)

5 Crayon resist (page 43)

6 Oil pastel glazing (page 32)

Resources

Most of the supplies used in this book are available from an art supply store, a hardware store, or an office supply store, or are things that you are likely to have around the house.

PAINTS AND ART SUPPLIES

Impress Me Rubber Stamps
(818) 788-6730
www.impressmenow.com

Brass Stencils
www.dreamweaverstencils.com

Faber Castell: Colored Pencils, Chalk, Watercolor Markers, and Oil Pastels
Art supply and craft stores

Gelli Plates
www.gelliarts.com

Jacquard Products: Fabric Paint, Dye-Na-flow, Cotton, Silk, Inkjet Fabric, Pearl Ex, Silkscreens, Silkscreen Ink, Dorland's Wax
Art supply and craft stores

Lutradur, TAP, InkTense
C&T publishing
www.ctpub.com

Liquitex Products: Molding Paste, Soft Body Acrylics, Gesso, Acrylic Media
Art supply and craft stores

Specialty Fiber Art Supplies and Silkscreens

Sherrill Kahn silkscreens, wax, printable tissue, brass stencils, yarns, pipettes, fusibles, threads, paint, unusual fabrics, needle felting supplies, cheesecloth, and other creative products

Meinke Toy
www.meinketoy.com

Staples Twist-Up Crayons
Staples office supply stores
www.staples.com

Textured and Decorative Paper Used in Collages
Black Ink Creative International Papers
www.gpcpapers.com

Thermofax Machines and Screens
www.welshproducts.com

FABRIC

Plain and Commercial Fabrics and Sherrill Kahn's Fabric Lines
Robert Kaufman Fabrics
www.robertkaufman.com

Sherrill Kahn fabrics are also available at www.equilter.com

MISCELLANEOUS SUPPLIES

Fun Foam
Hobby and craft stores

Metal Tape and Wallboard Grid Tape
Home improvement and hardware stores

About the Author

Sherrill Kahn was a public school teacher for the Los Angeles Unified School District for 30 years, including 27 years at Palisades High School, teaching drawing, painting, fiber art, and design. Since retiring, she has become an internationally known mixed-media artist, teaching her colorful techniques throughout the United States and Canada, and also in Australia, England, India, Switzerland, and Germany.

Sherrill has written 7 books and more than 50 magazine articles featuring her ever-expanding range of expressive techniques. She has been on *The Carol Duvall Show* twice and has created a DVD featuring her art techniques.

Her art has been used in many products, including six lines of fabrics from Robert Kaufman Fabrics; Rollagraph stamps from Clearsnap; and many rubber stamps from her company, Impress Me.

Sherrill loves to share her techniques with others and lives by the words "what if."

Great Titles and Products

from C&T PUBLISHING

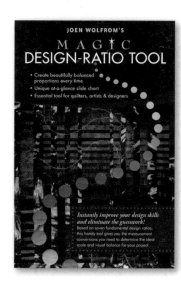

Available at your local retailer or **www.ctpub.com** *or* **800-284-1114**